# COLOR
## YouR WAy

A COLOR JOURNAL + QUOTES AND AFFIRMATIONS

*Thank you so much for always supporting me. You are my sunshine, Wanda. Live life in color!*

*xoxo
Lisa Renee*

**LIFE IS ART. LIVE YOURS IN COLOR.**

-Anonymous

# COLOR Your WAy

A COLOR JOURNAL + QUOTES AND AFFIRMATIONS

## LISA RENEE JOHNSON

Brown Girl Press

Brown Girl Press

Copyright © 2018 by Lisa Renee Johnson
All rights reserved. This book or any portion thereof
may not be reproduced or used in any manner whatsoever
without the express written permission of the publisher.

Artwork designed by Maria Silvo

Printed in the United States of America

First Printing, 2018

ISBN 978-0-9892418-1-6

Brown Girl Press
201 Sand Creek Road Suite L-B
Brentwood, CA 94513

www.lisareneejohnson.com

# Also by

## LISA RENEE JOHNSON

Coming Soon

dangerous
consequences
LISA RENEE
JOHNSON

Dangerous Consequences

surviving
the chase
LISA RENEE
JOHNSON

Surviving the Chase

eBook, paperback, audiobook available
where books are sold.

# introduction

Welcome to Color Your Way!

This book contains quotes and affirmations to get you inspired, journal pages for reflective practice and beautiful illustrations just waiting for you to bring them to life with your imagination. This is my invitation to you to relax and begin you very own personal journey of creative expression.

My hope is that "Color Your Way." is the spark that ignites your creativity and inner artist to live your life out loud and to color your "brick road" any color you choose.

What you need to get started:
1. Open mind to explore the depths of you.
2. Pen that you enjoy writing with "sunshine pen"
3. Colored pens, pencils, or crayons that you like to color with. Note: color markers may bleed through the page.

**Ready, Set, COLOR More!**

## free gift for you

Living the life you deserve doesn't just happen. You have to create it. Start by downloading this FREE tool to get the clarity you need to live your best life now.

Flower of Life

Flower of Life

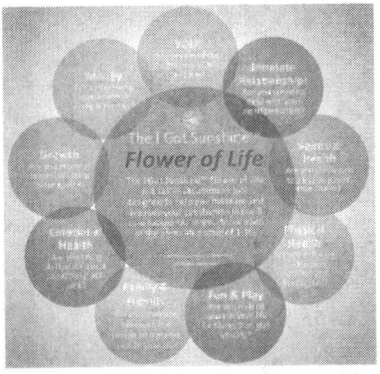

http://www.lisareneejohnson.com/folsubscribe

## Let's keep in touch

www.lisareneejohnson.com

@iamlisareneejohnson

community

www.shinebrighter.me

*sometimes all you need is a little splash of*

# COLOR

FOUR LITTLE WORDS:

# what's your favorite color?

color me your fav!

# color play

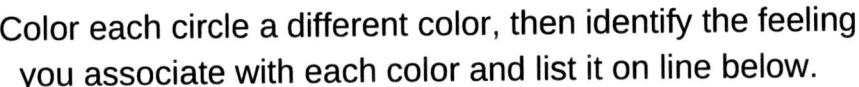

Color each circle a different color, then identify the feeling you associate with each color and list it on line below.

# I AM *enough*

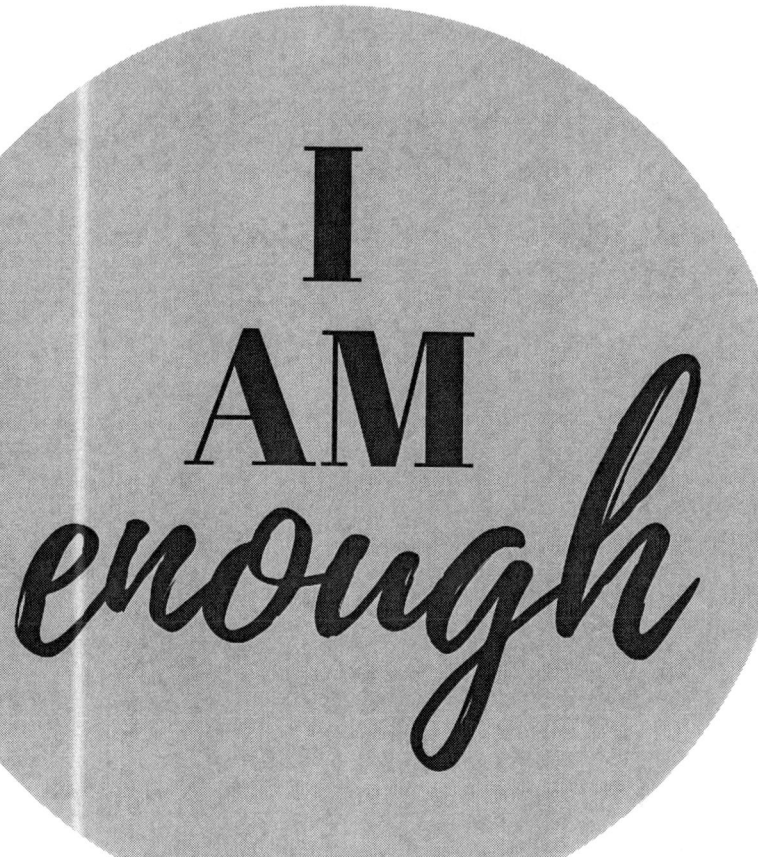

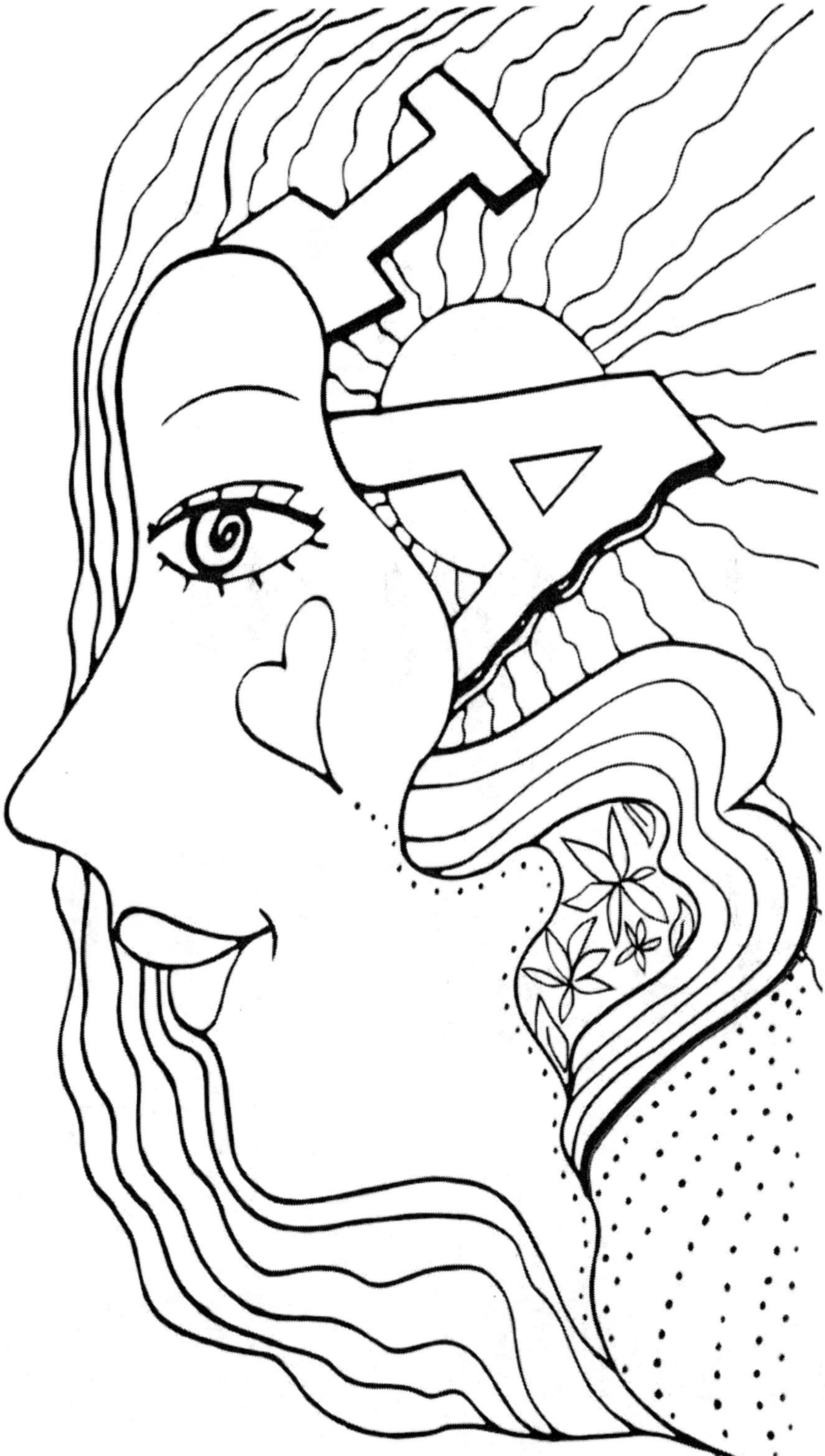

# KNOW Your W❋RTH

...then add TAX

# write it down

What key life moments define who you are today?

# Broken crayons still color.

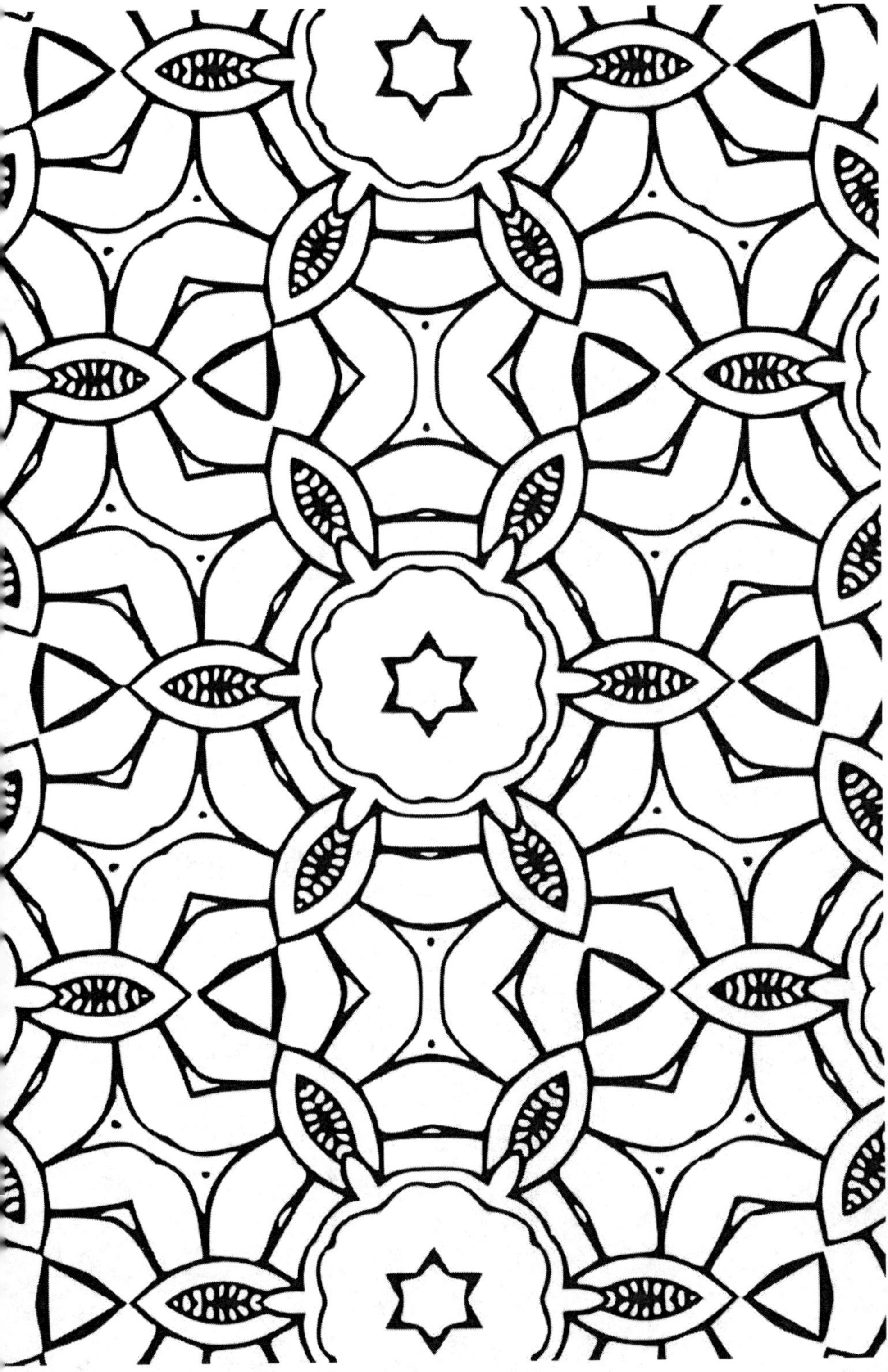

the greatest source of happiness is the ability to be grateful at all times.

-Zig Ziglar

# write it down

## What are you most grateful for in your life?

EVERYTHING

I WANT IS

ON THE

OTHER SIDE

OF FEAR.

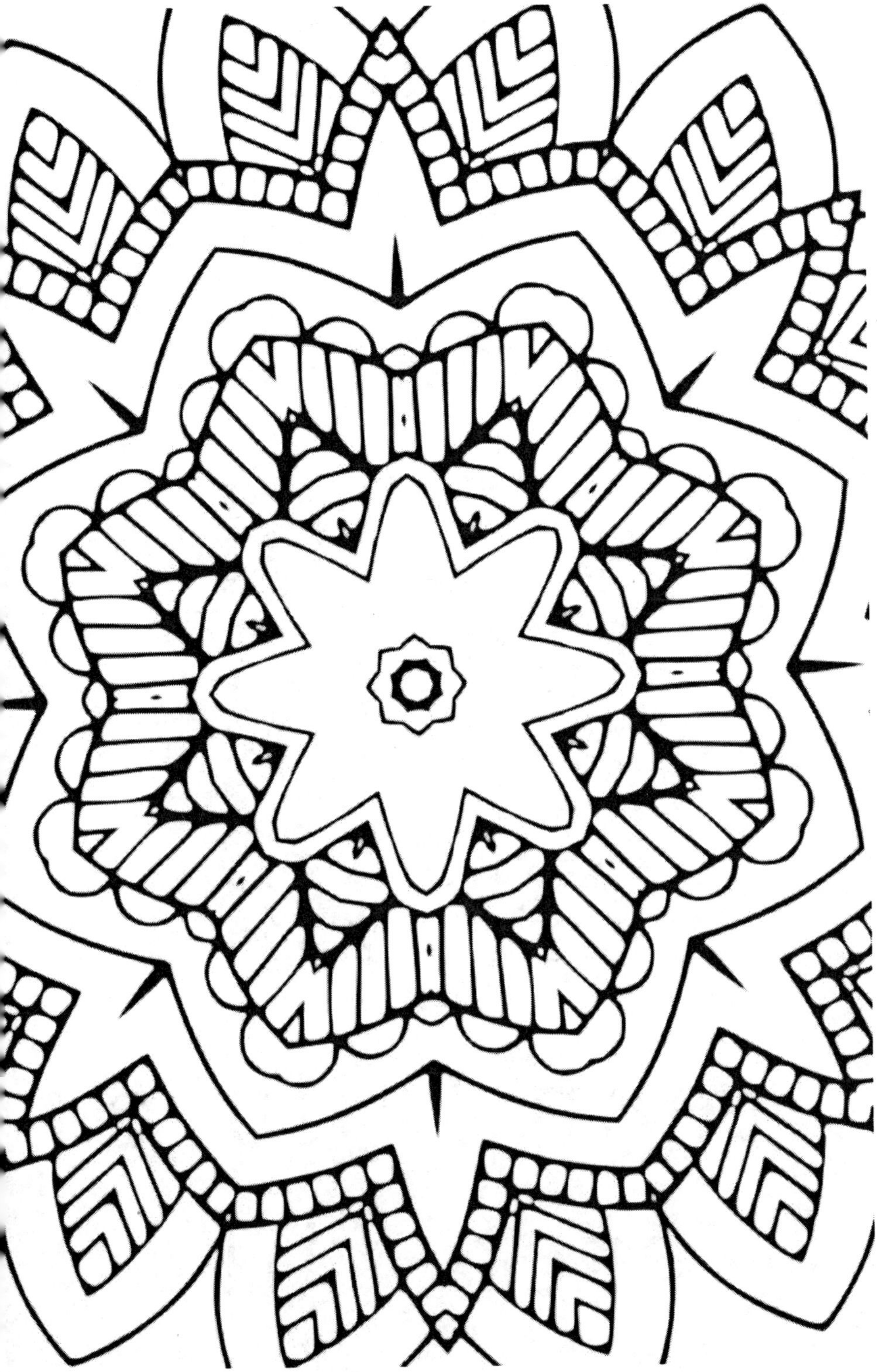

# FEAR kills more dreams

than failure ever will.

# write it down

What would you do if you weren't afraid?

# LIVE THE WAY YOU WANT TO BE REMEMBERED

# What is your BIG Why?

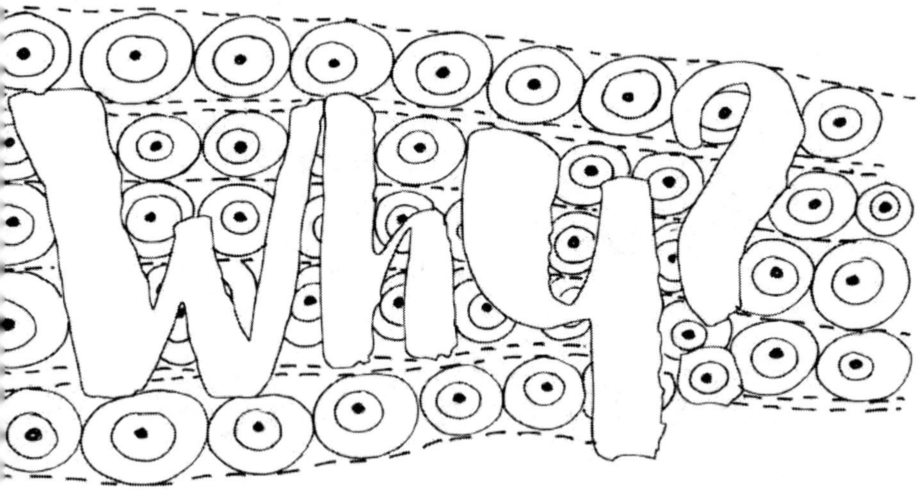

Why?

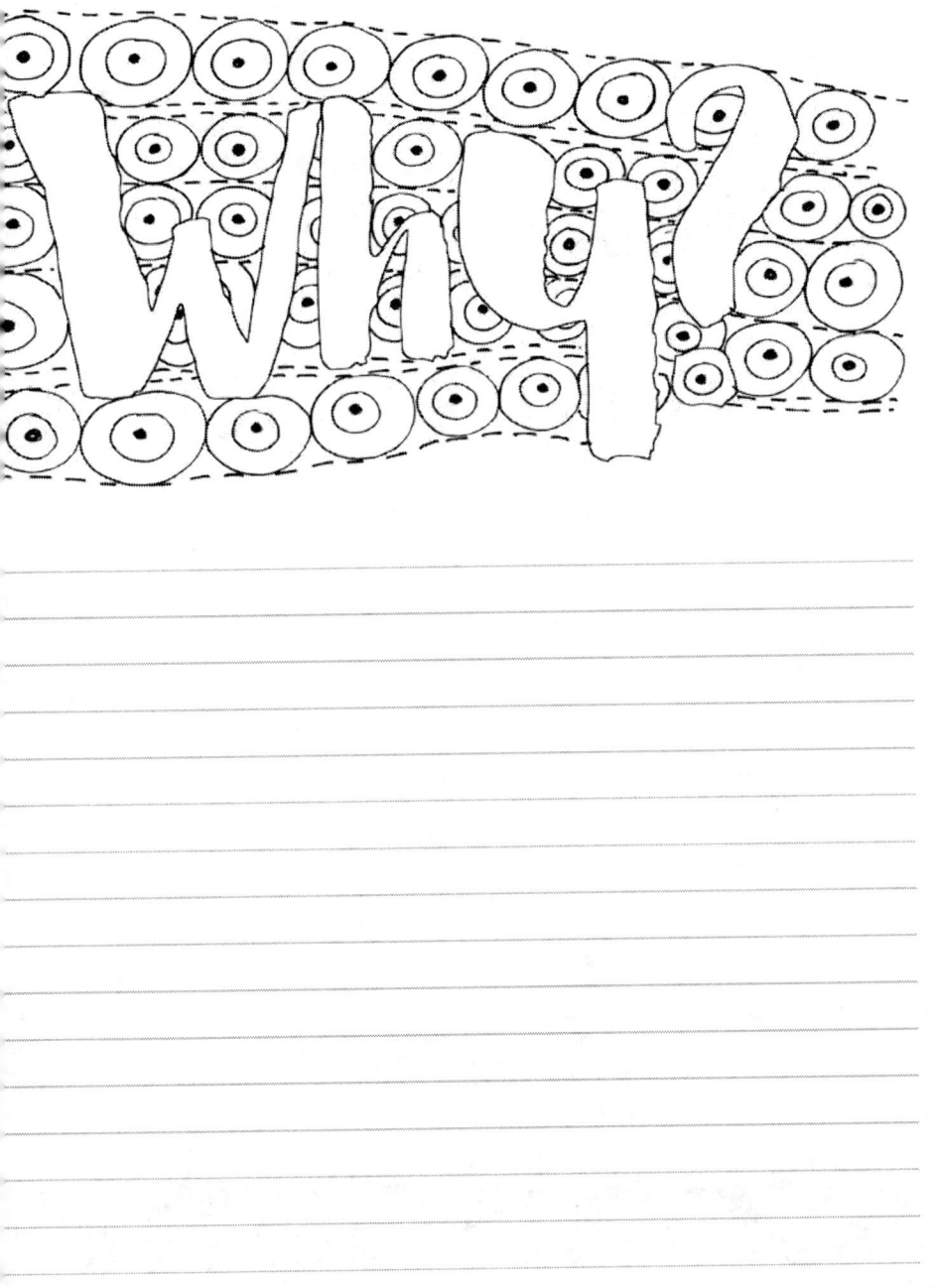

I FEEL

mindful

*Powerful*

relaxed

**ADVENTUROUS**

SATISFIED  intuitive

beautiful

strong  grateful

*brave*  **LOVED**

CAPABLE

*motivated*  unique

**Confident**

# write it down

## What makes you feel powerful?

"a person can, by assuming two simple one-minute poses, embody power and instantly become more powerful."

-Amy Cuddy

# I AM STRONG
Because I know my weakness.

# I AM BEAUTIFUL
Because I embrace my flaws.

# I AM FEARLESS
Because I recognize illusion from real.

# I AM WISE
Because I learn from my mistakes.

# I AM LOVE
Because I have felt hate.

# I LAUGH OUT LOUD
Because I decided not to stay silent.

# write it down

What does unconditional self-love look like for you?

Never chase love, affection or attention. If it isn't given freely by another person it isn't worth having.

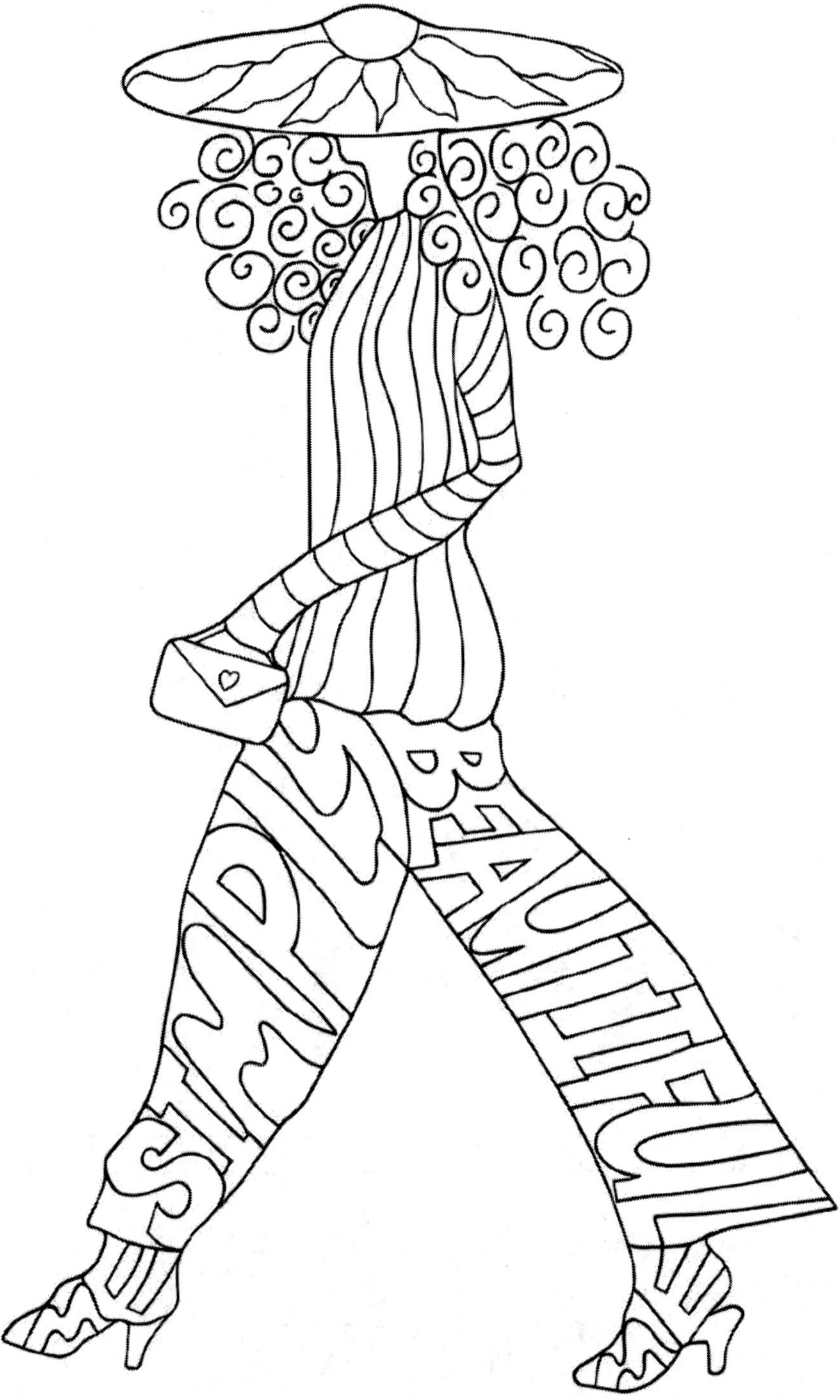
SIMPLY
BEAUTIFUL

# LOVE
*what you do.*

# DO
*what you love.*

# PASSION
is the key that opens the door to JOY and ABUNDANCE.

# write it down

When do you feel like your most authentic self? What are you doing? Who are you doing it with?

Beauty is being the best possible version of yourself on the inside and out.

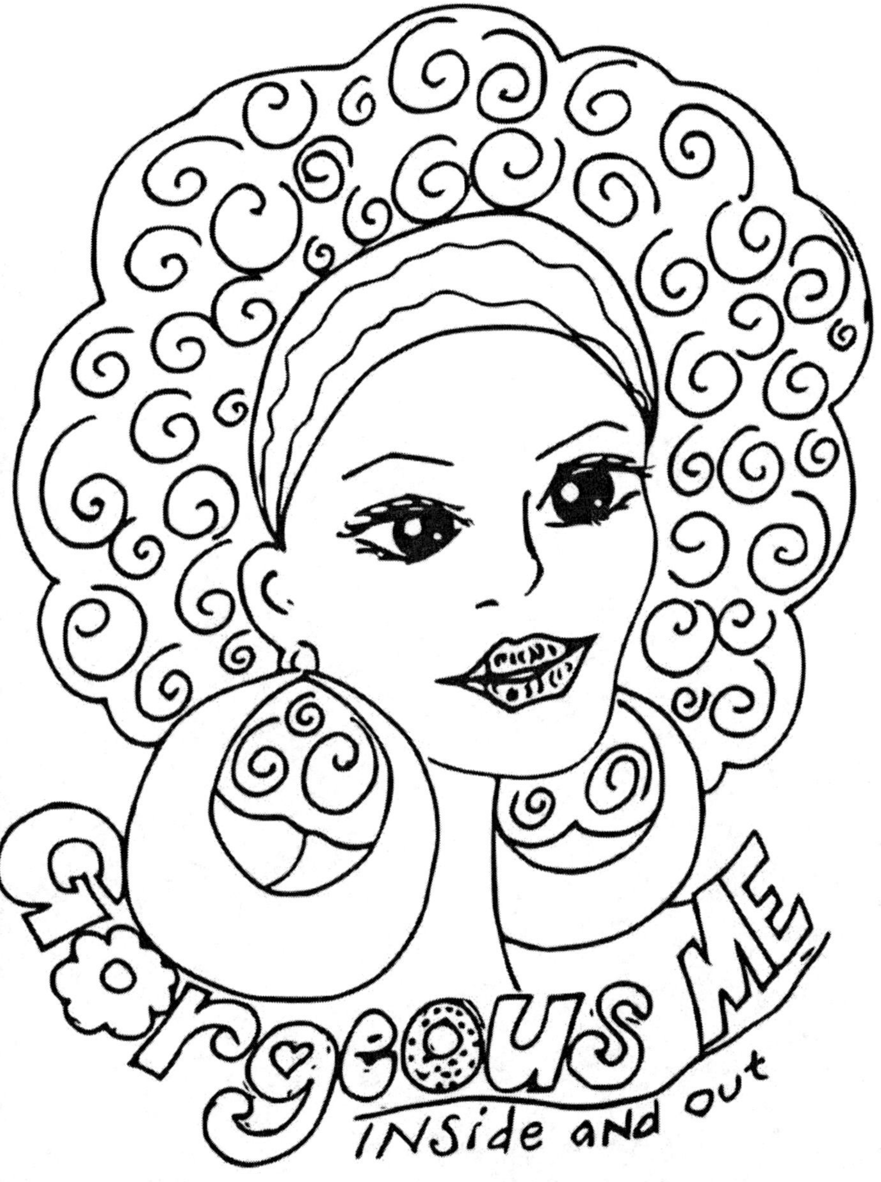

Gorgeous ME
INSide and out

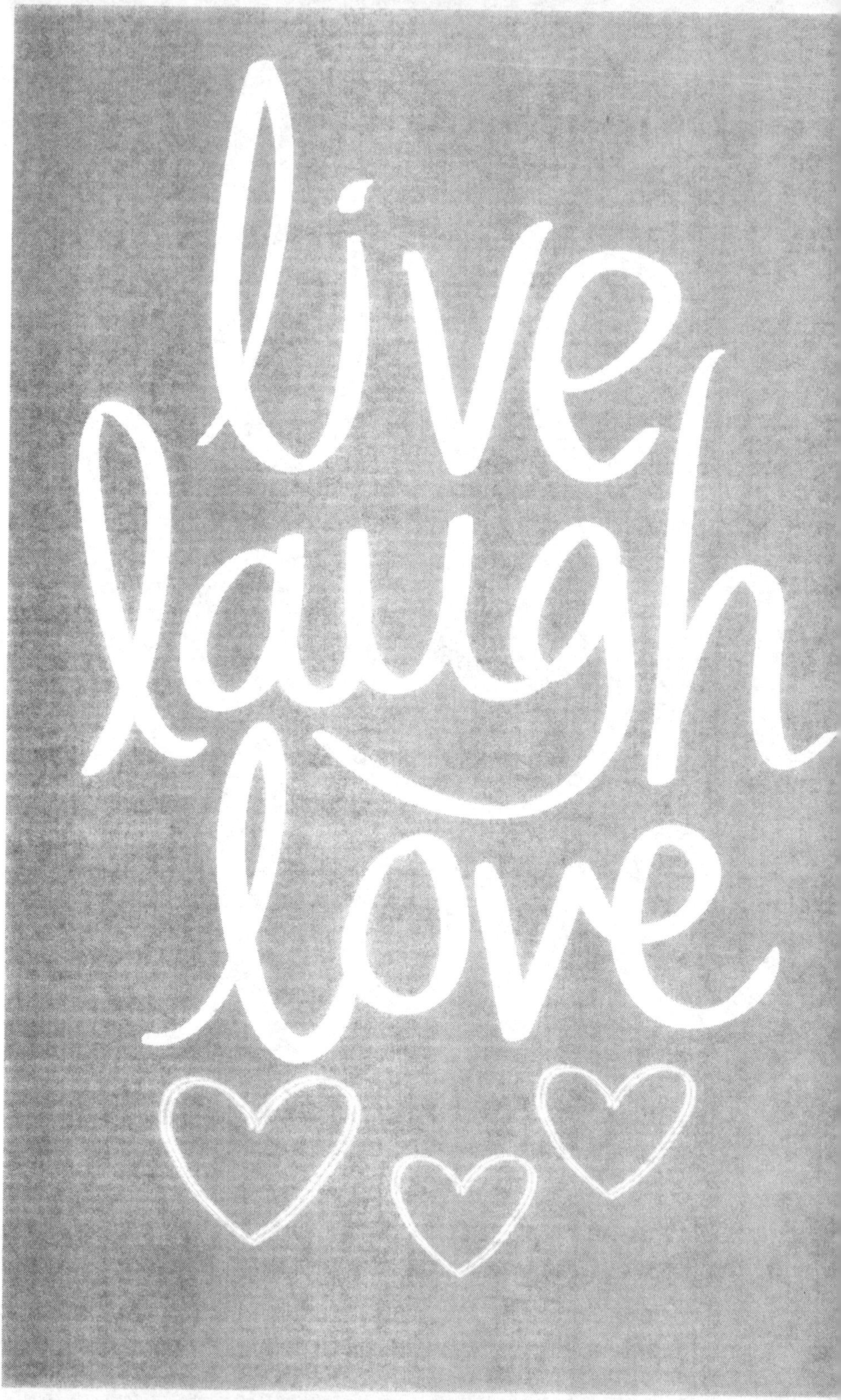
live
laugh
love

# write it down

Who inspires you with their passion and purpose? Why?

# Embrace
the
## COLOR
in

**black and white**

**spaces.**

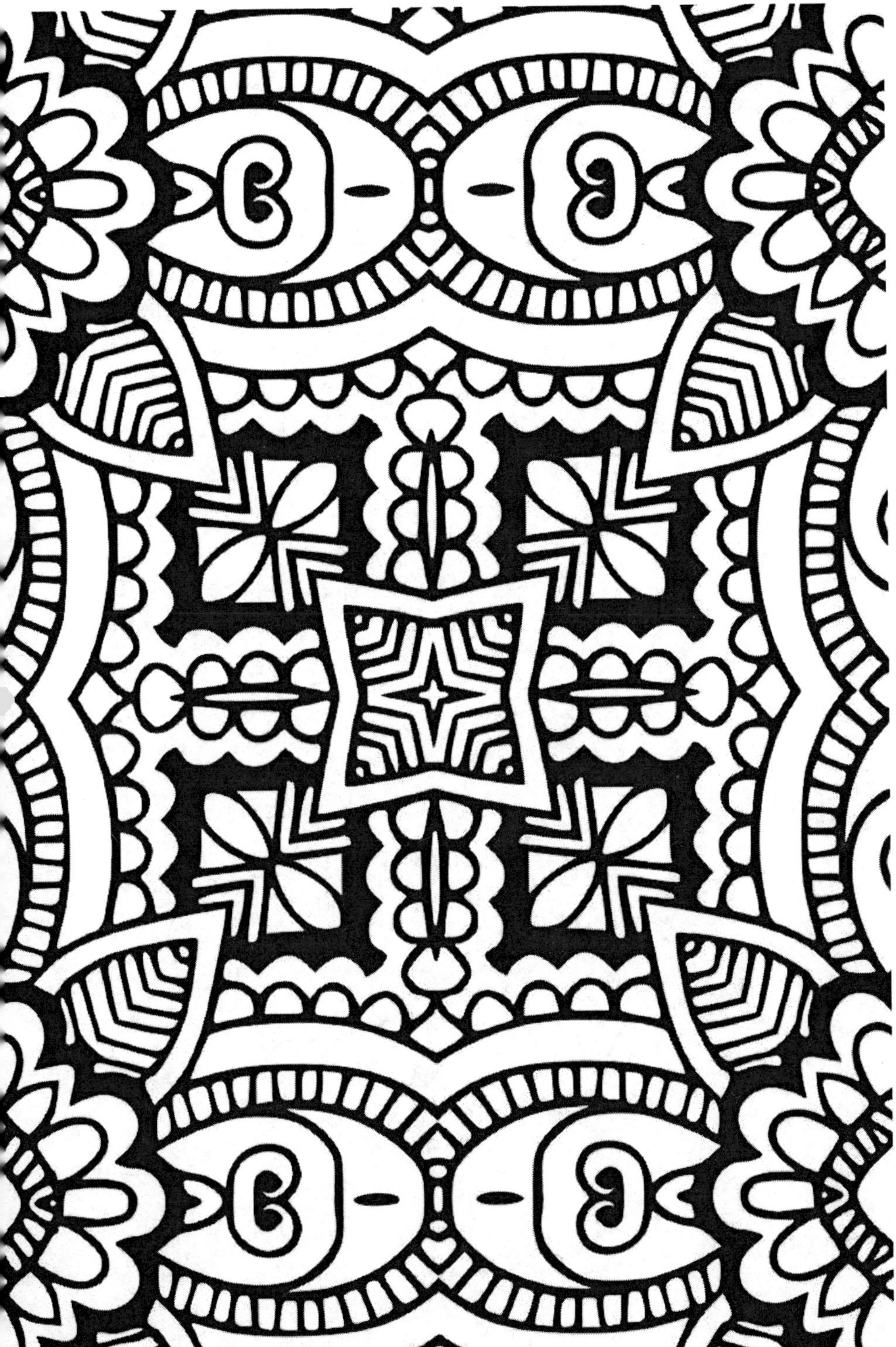

# MOVE! GET OUT OF YOUR OWN WAY.

# write it down

What is standing in the way of you realizing your hopes and dreams?

# EVERY FLOWER MUST GROW THROUGH DIRT.

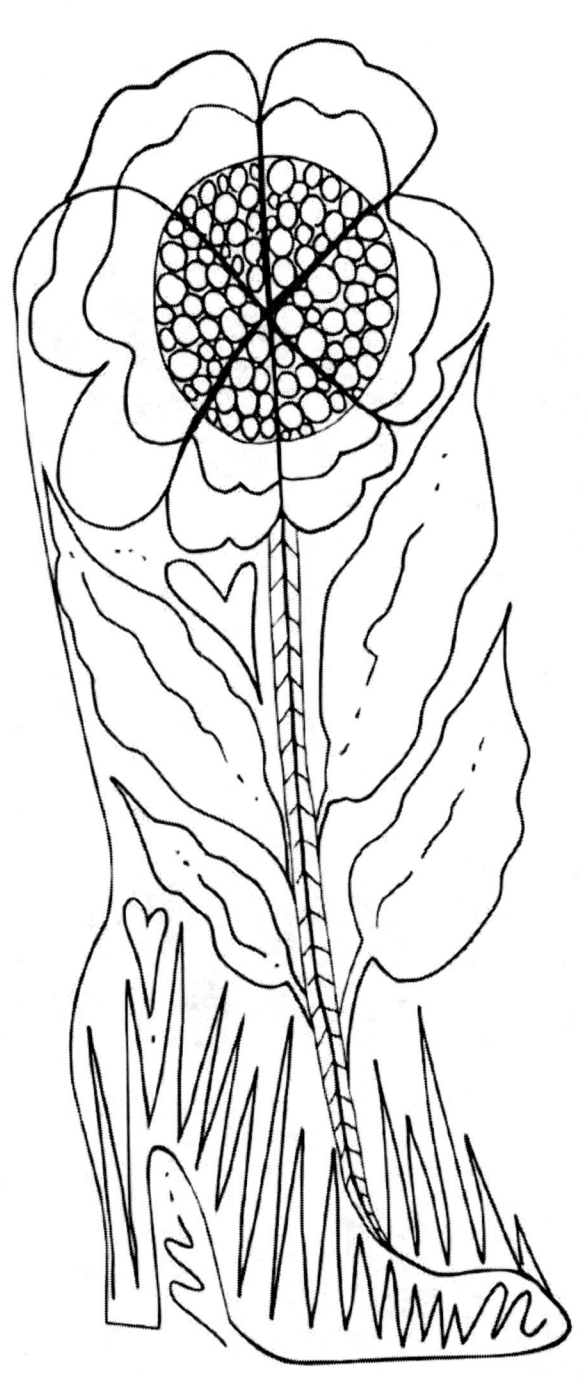

I AM THE

# *Hero*

of my own

# Story.

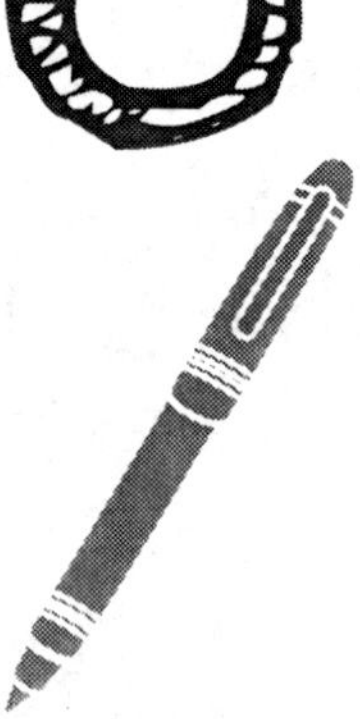

I hold the pen.

# write it down

When do you feel the most at peace?

The soul becomes dyed with the COLOR of its thoughts.

-Marcus Aureleus

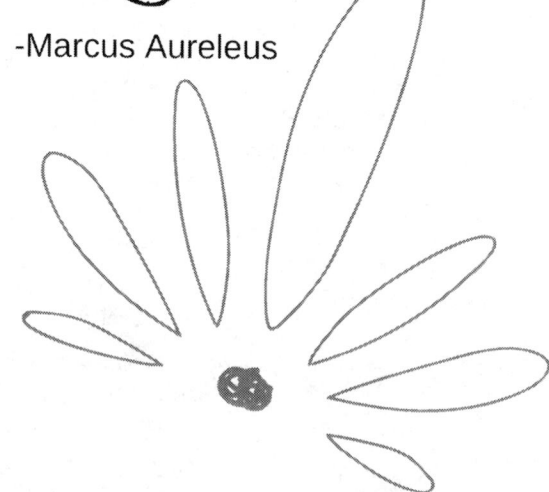

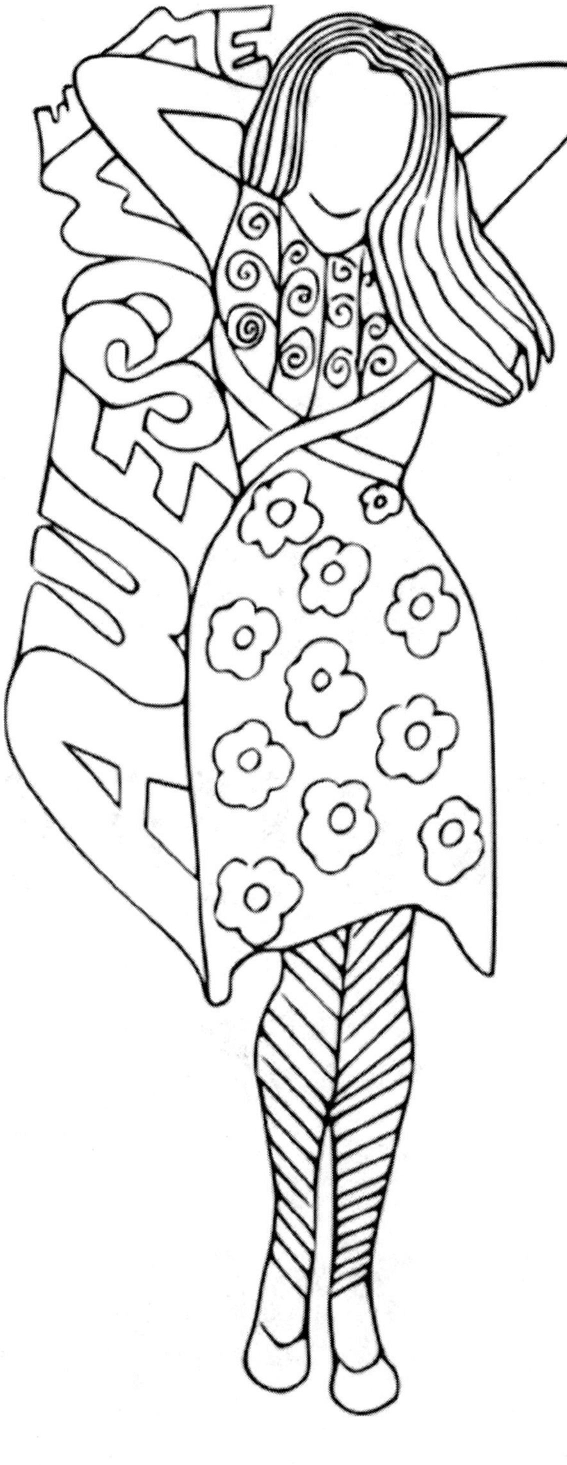
AWESOME ME

# BE THE BEST VERSION OF YOU!

# write it down

## What do you want to be known for?

# EVERYBODY LOVES THE

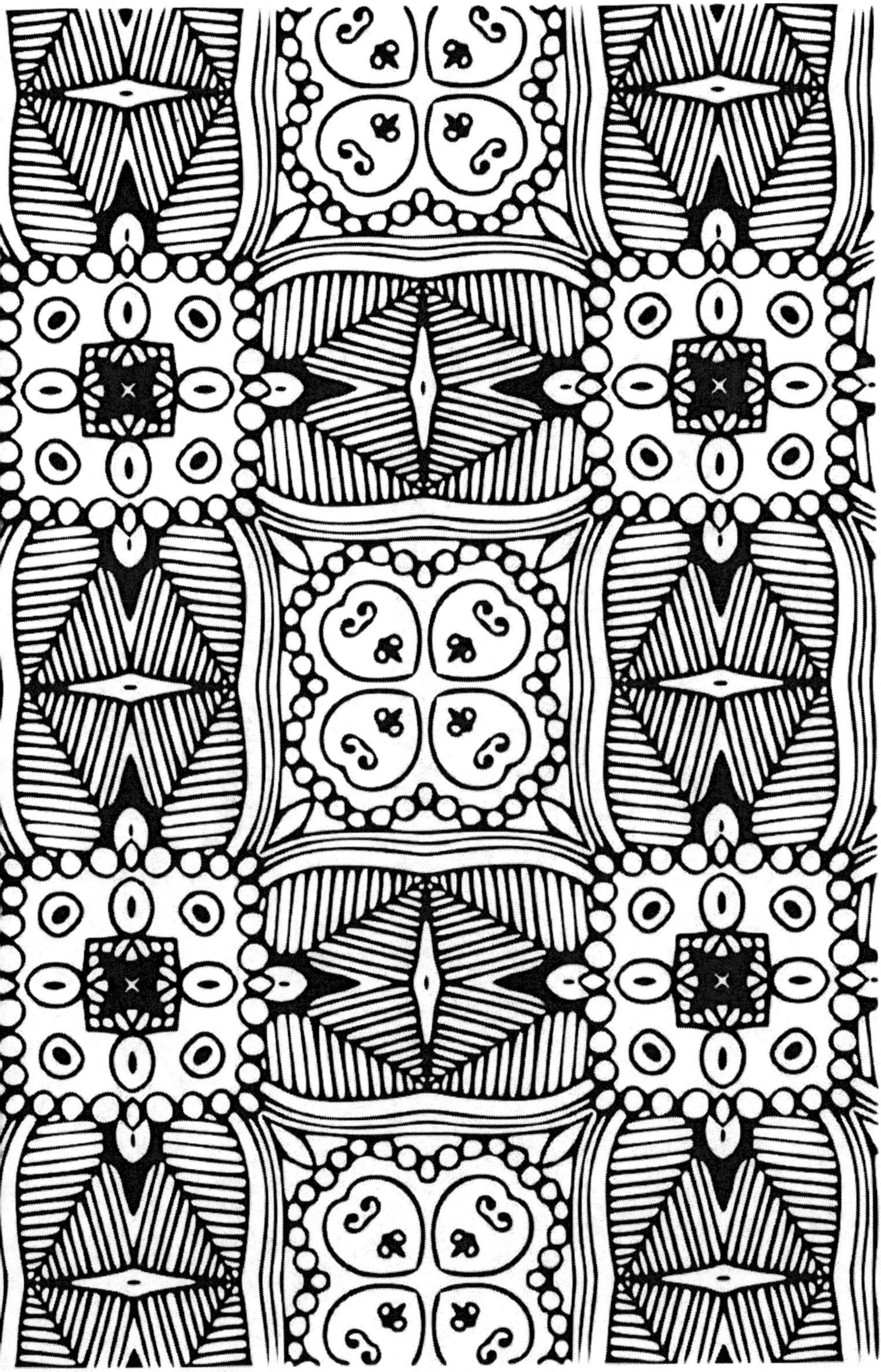

# DREAM
# BIG

# write it down

## How do you feed your spirit?

your abundance is

directly correlated

to what you

believe.

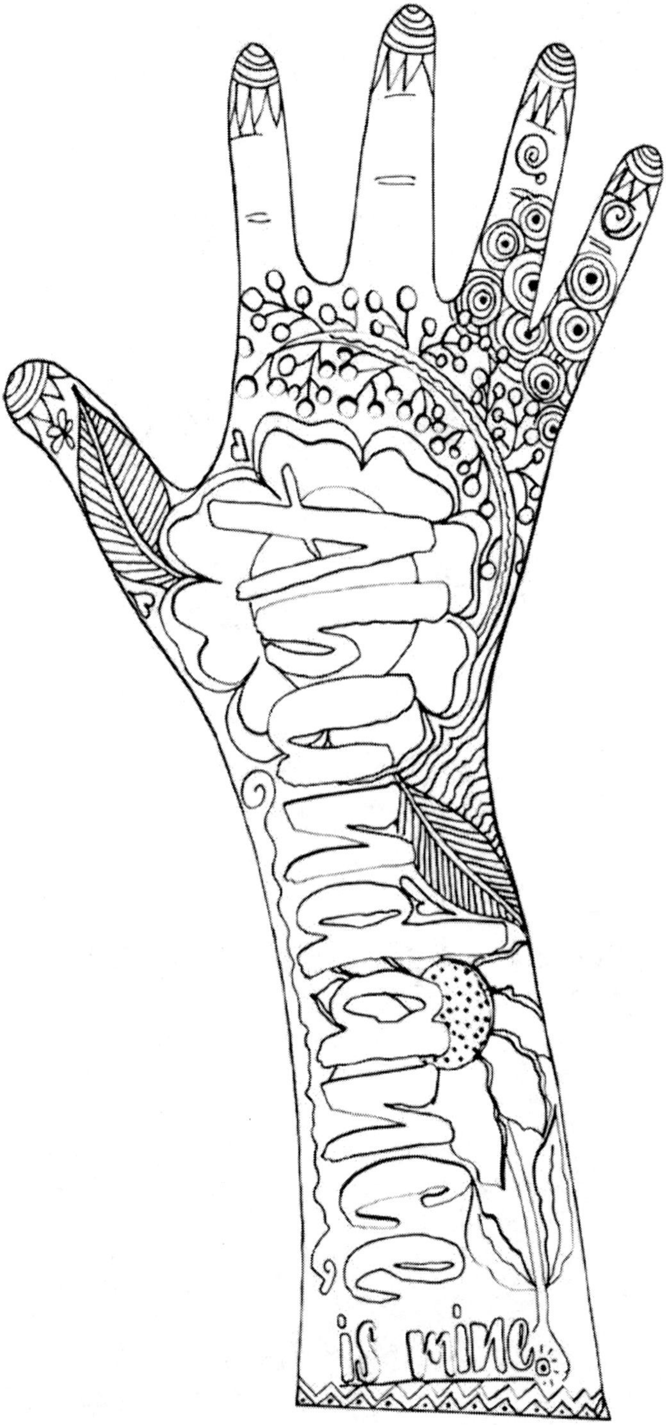
Awesome
is mine.

Never Let a
Stumble
in the Road
Be The
End of
Your Journey.

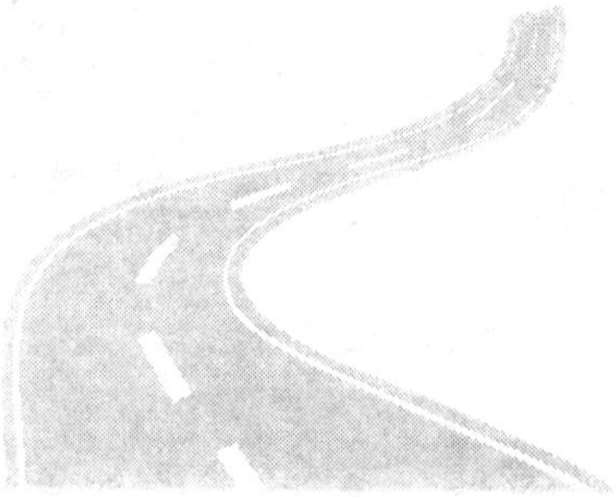

# write it down

What is your truth today?

be fearless in the pursuit of what sets your soul on fire.

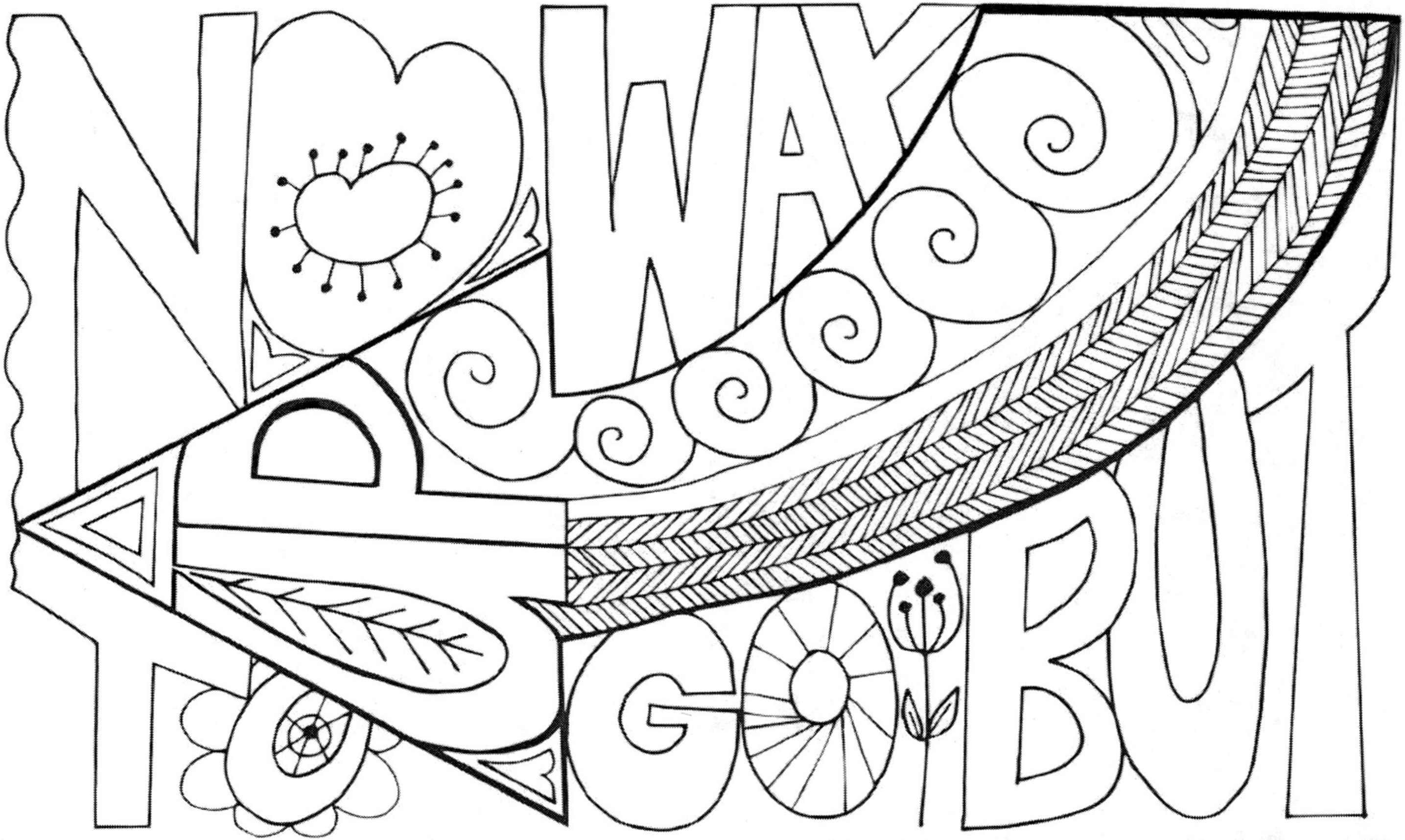
NO WAY
TO
UP
GO BUT

# YOU
*don't have to be*

## PERFECT

*to be*

## AMAZING.

# write it down

Write a love note to yourself.

# today
♥
## i am
# EXCITED
## about...

# Sometimes you gotta fall before you FLY.

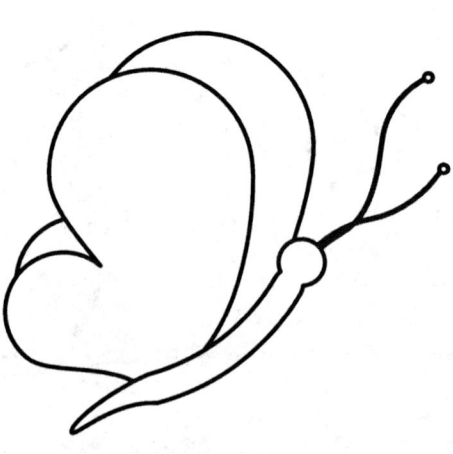

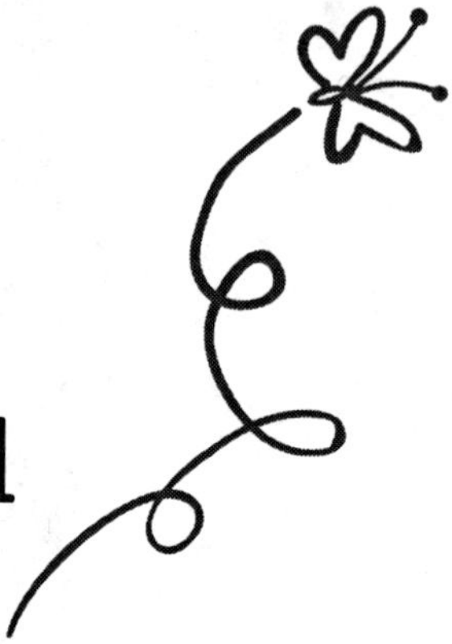

# write it down

What do you want your life to look and feel like?

The best project I will ever work on is **ME.**

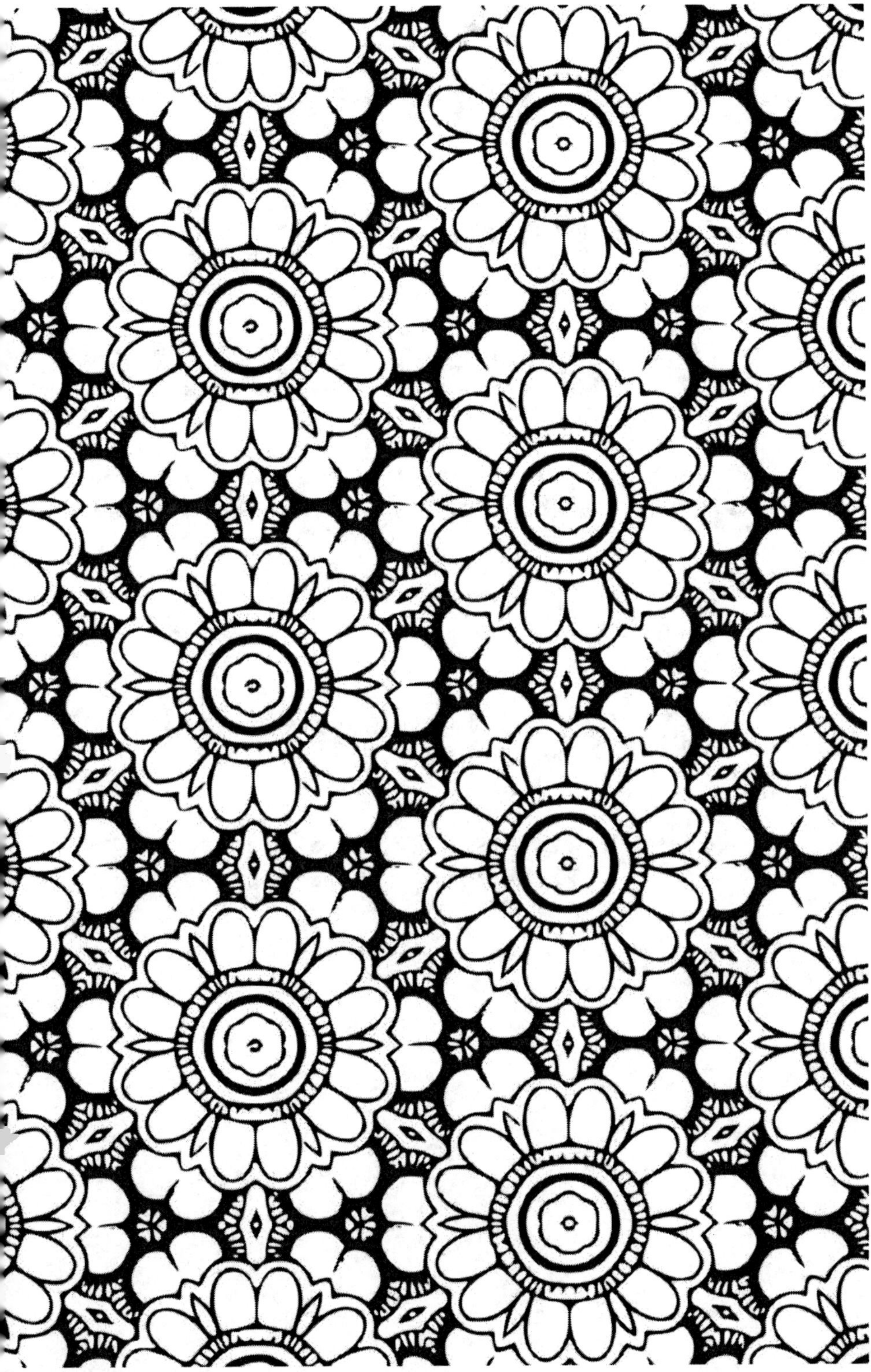

# STOP
# being afraid of what could go wrong and get excited about what can go right.

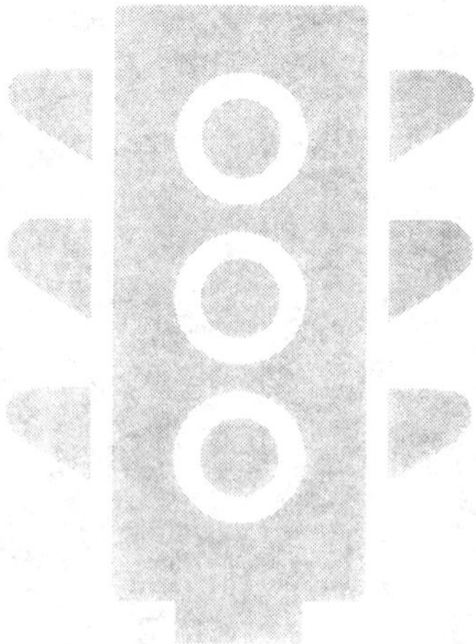

# write it down

What do you value in yourself? What do you value in other people?

IF YOU WANT TO GIVE LIGHT TO OTHERS YOU HAVE TO SHINE YOURSELF.

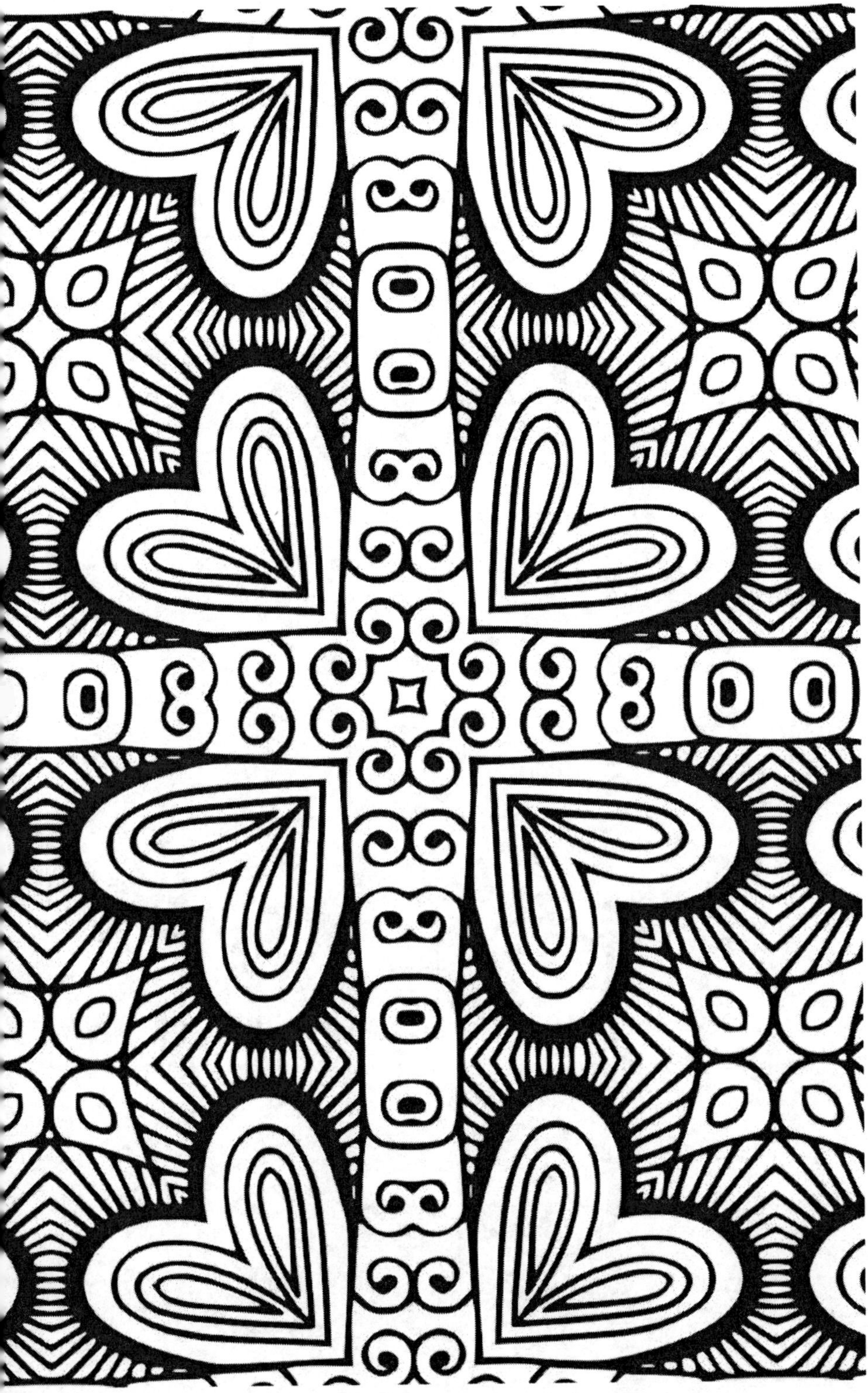

you are

*What*

you

Think

# write it down

## How do you show up in the world?

"If I didn't define myself for myself, I would be crunched into other people's fantasies for me and eaten alive."

-Audre Lorde

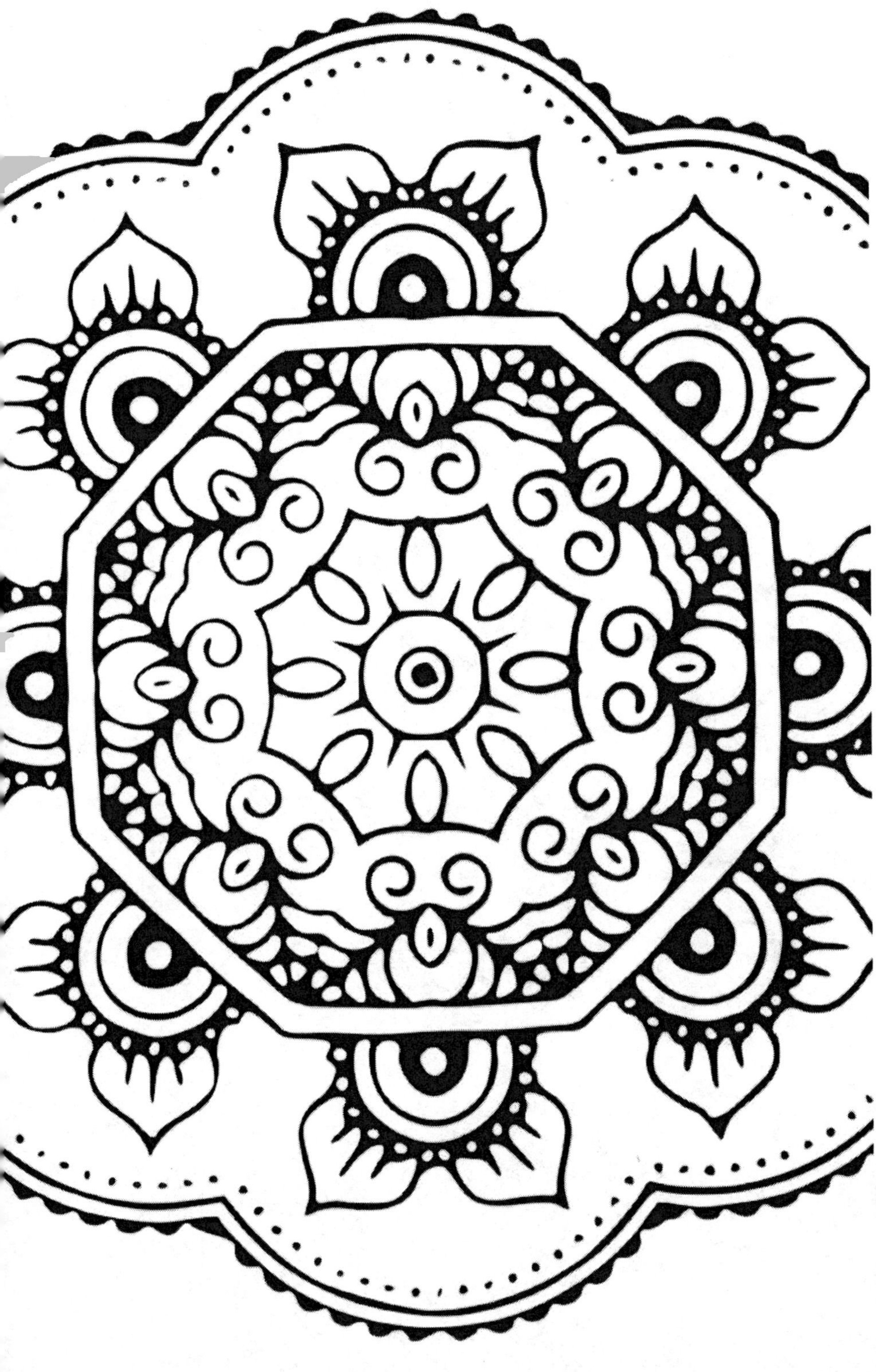

# I AM:

- [ ] *beautiful*
- [ ] *strong*
- [ ] *worthy*
- [ ] *important*
- [ ] *chosen*
- [ ] *love*

# write it down

## What does joy look like in your life?

"Your crown has been bought and paid for. Put it on your head and wear it."

-Maya Angelou

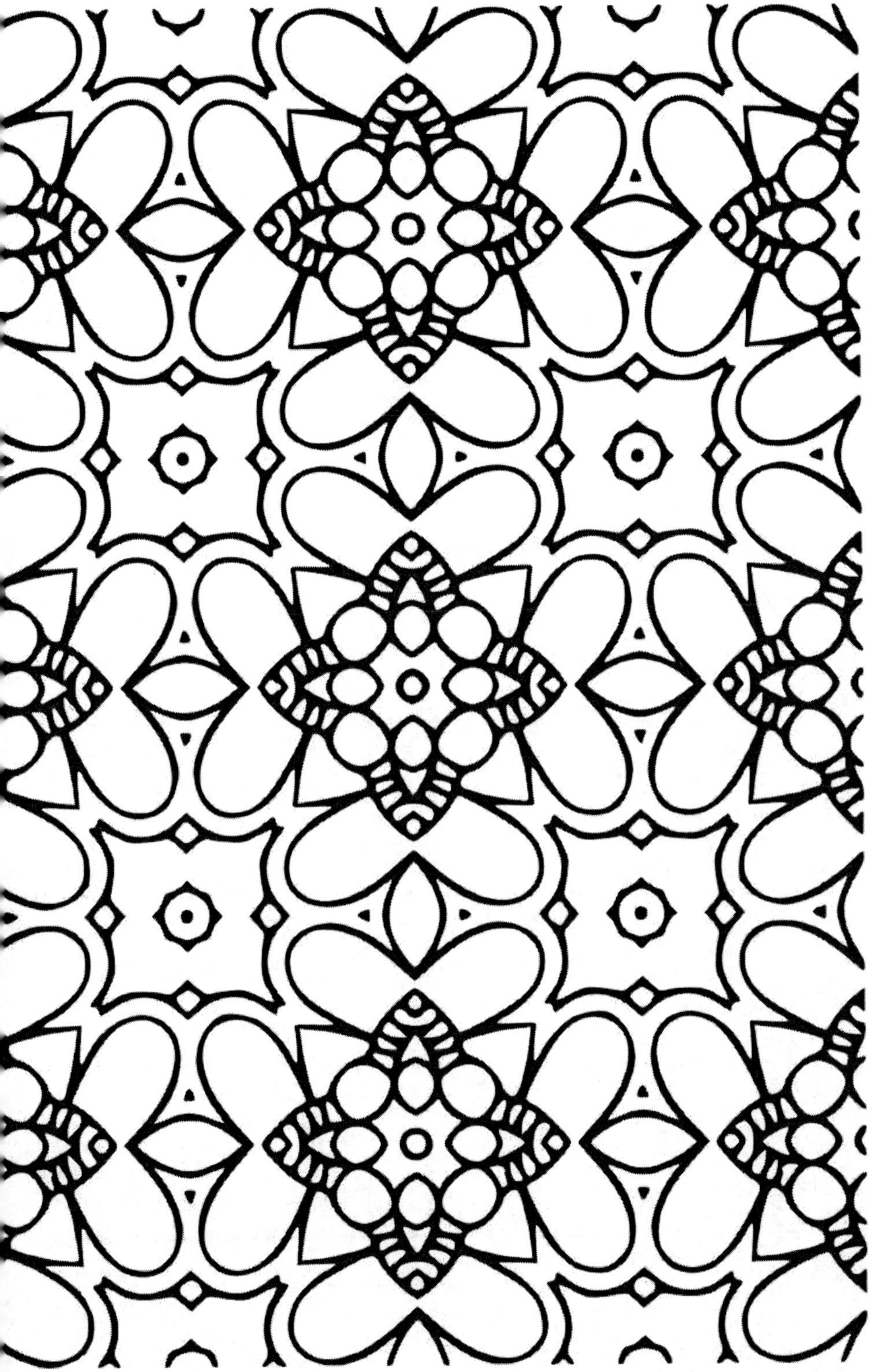

# I AM

_____

_____

_____

_____

_____

# write it down

Where do I want to be one year from now financially?

i am

perfectly

imperfect.

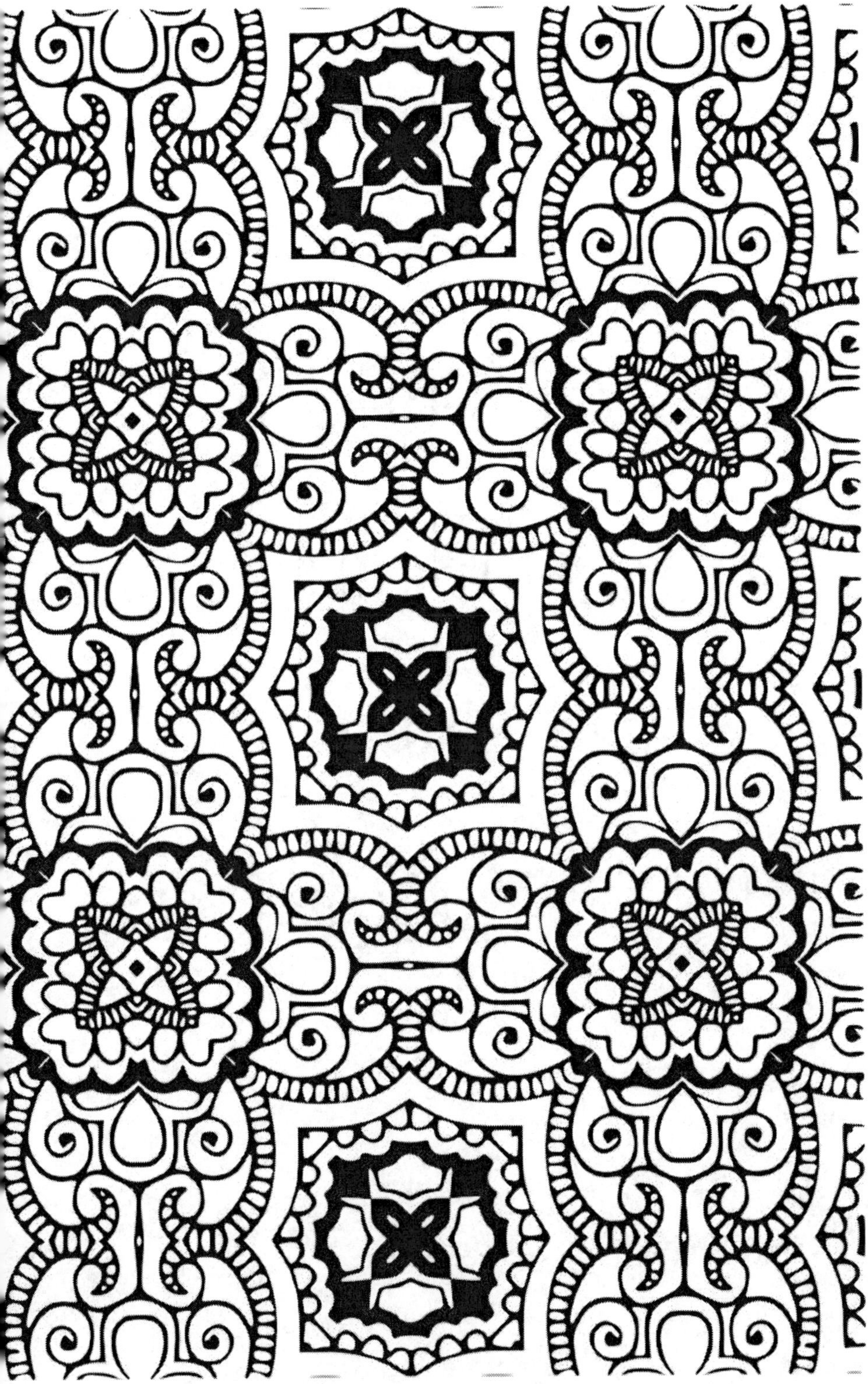

Don't Judge My "Breakthrough" Until You Know My "Been-Through."

# write it down

What's the biggest blockage you have overcome in your health, relationships, family, finances, business or other area of your life?

I choose

happiness,

success

and

abundance

in

my life.

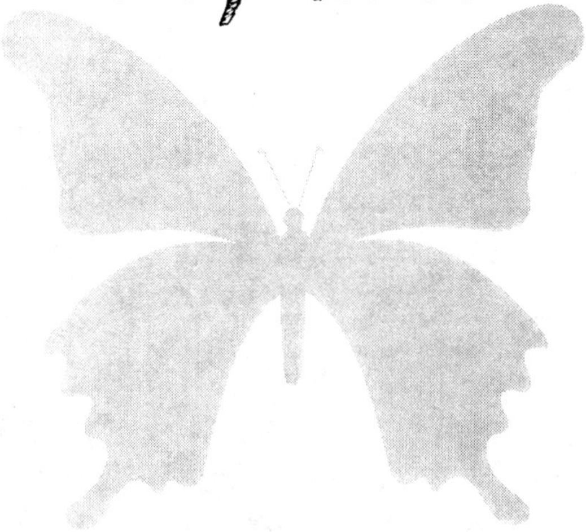

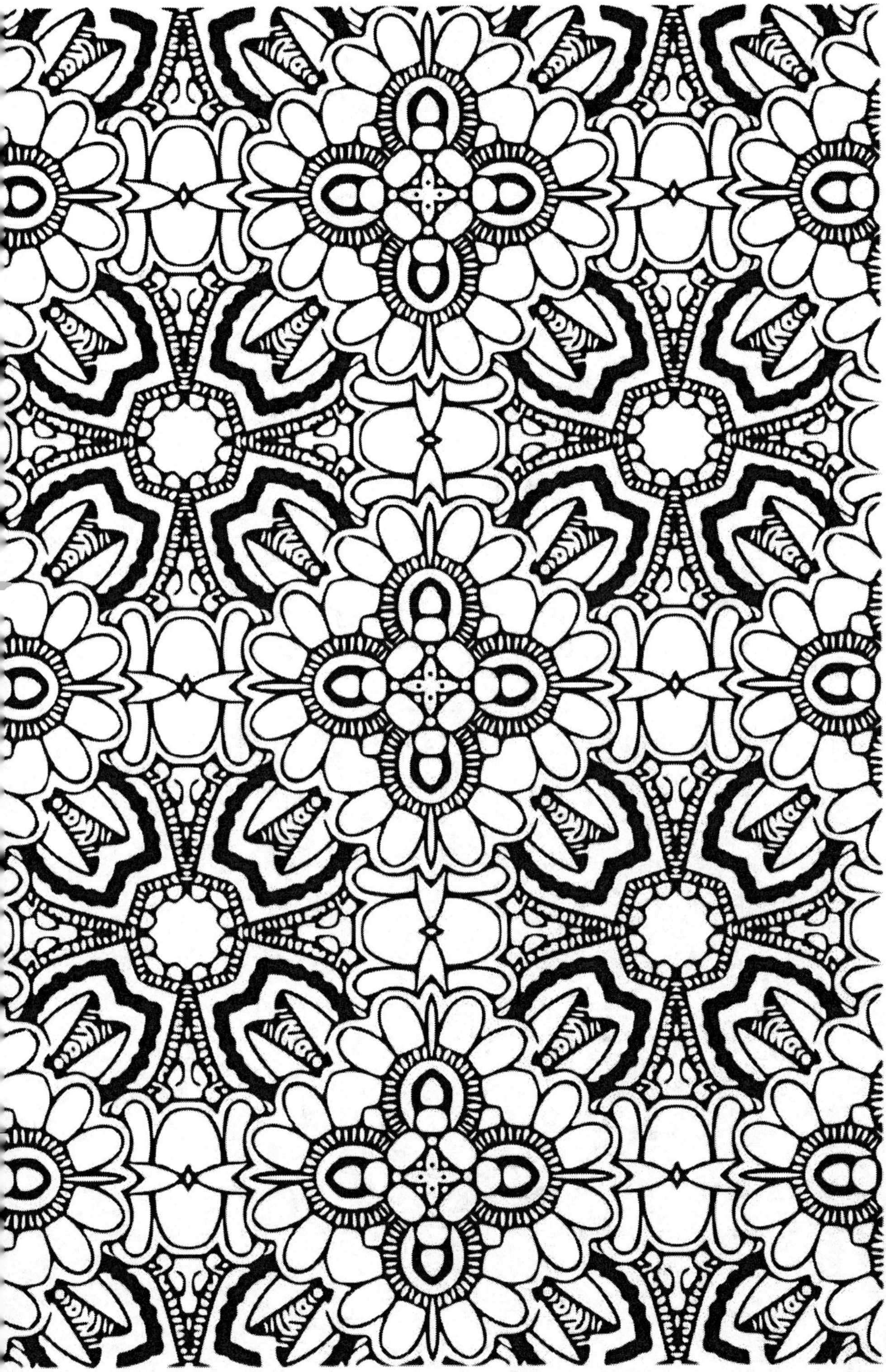

"The Sunshine Life doesn't just happen. You have to create it."

# write it down

## When do you feel your happiest?

**FORGIVENESS** is an act of **SELF + love**

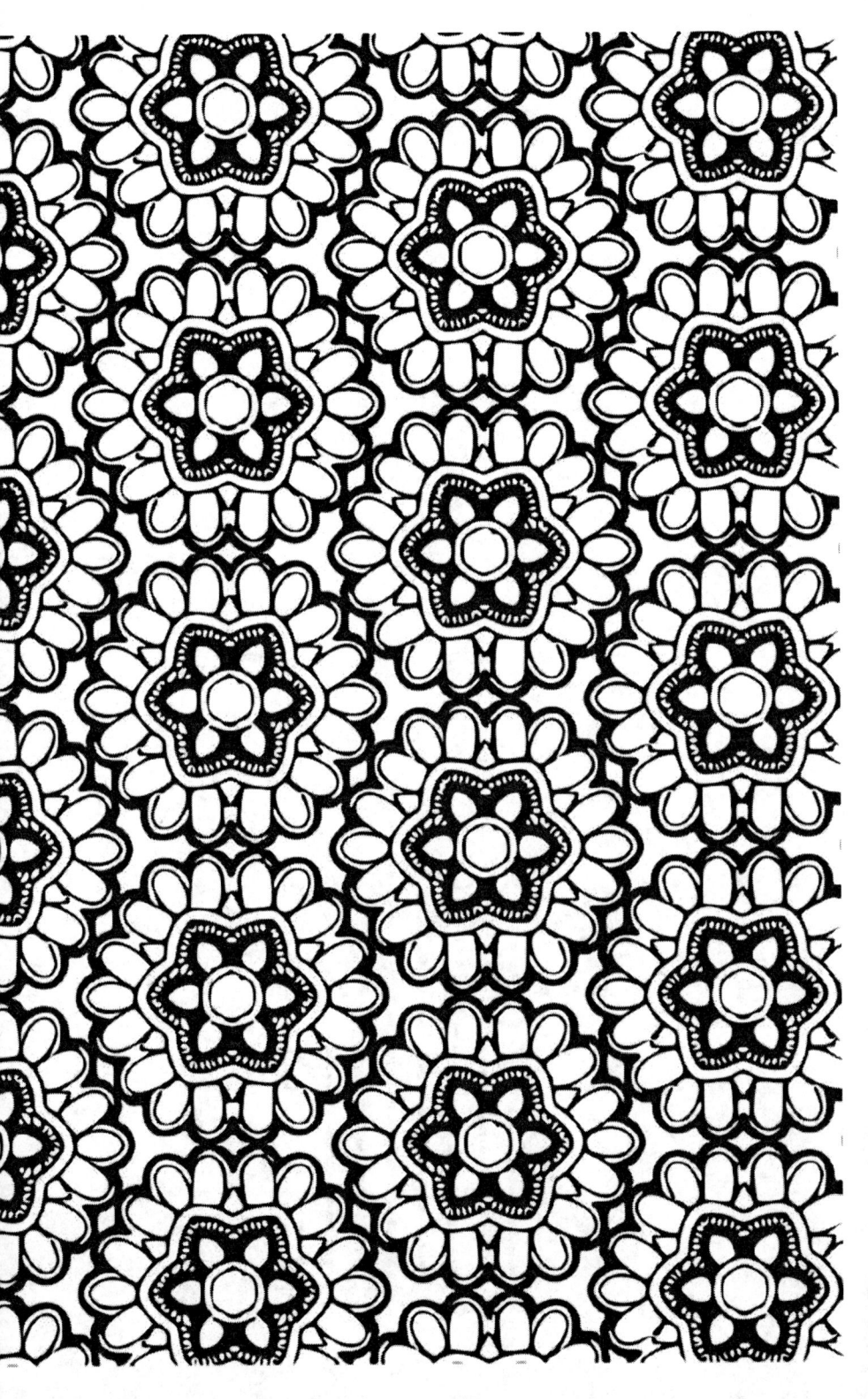

# I ALWAYS have a Choice.

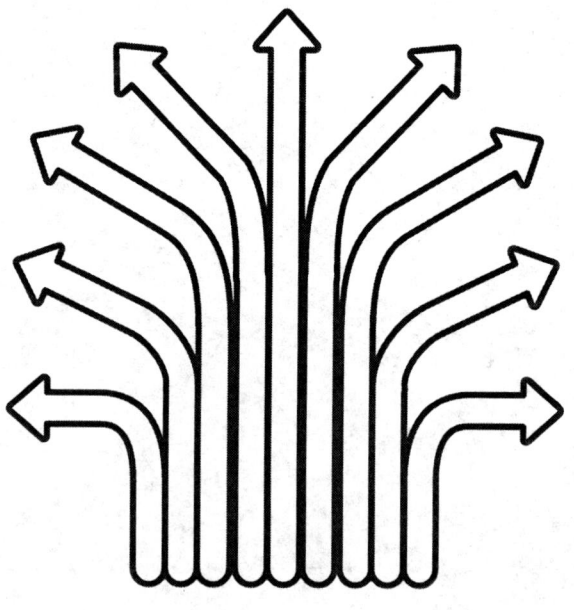

# write it down

## What excuses do you need to stop making?

# Put Your Positive Dress

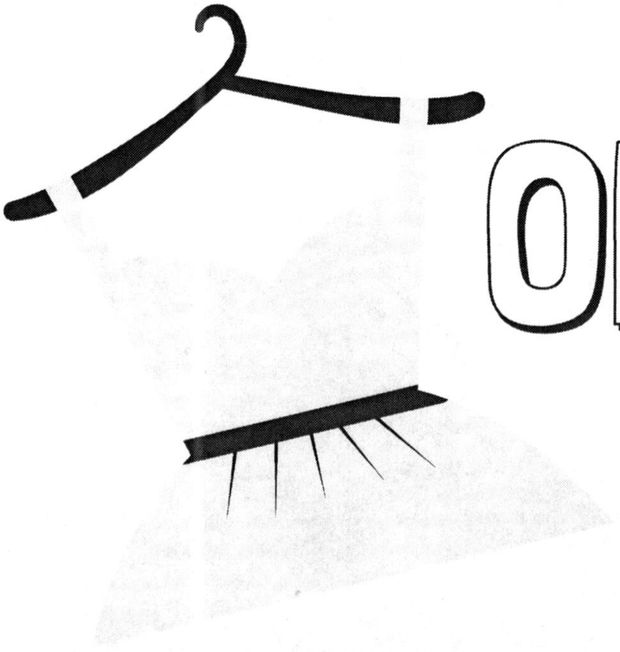

# ON!

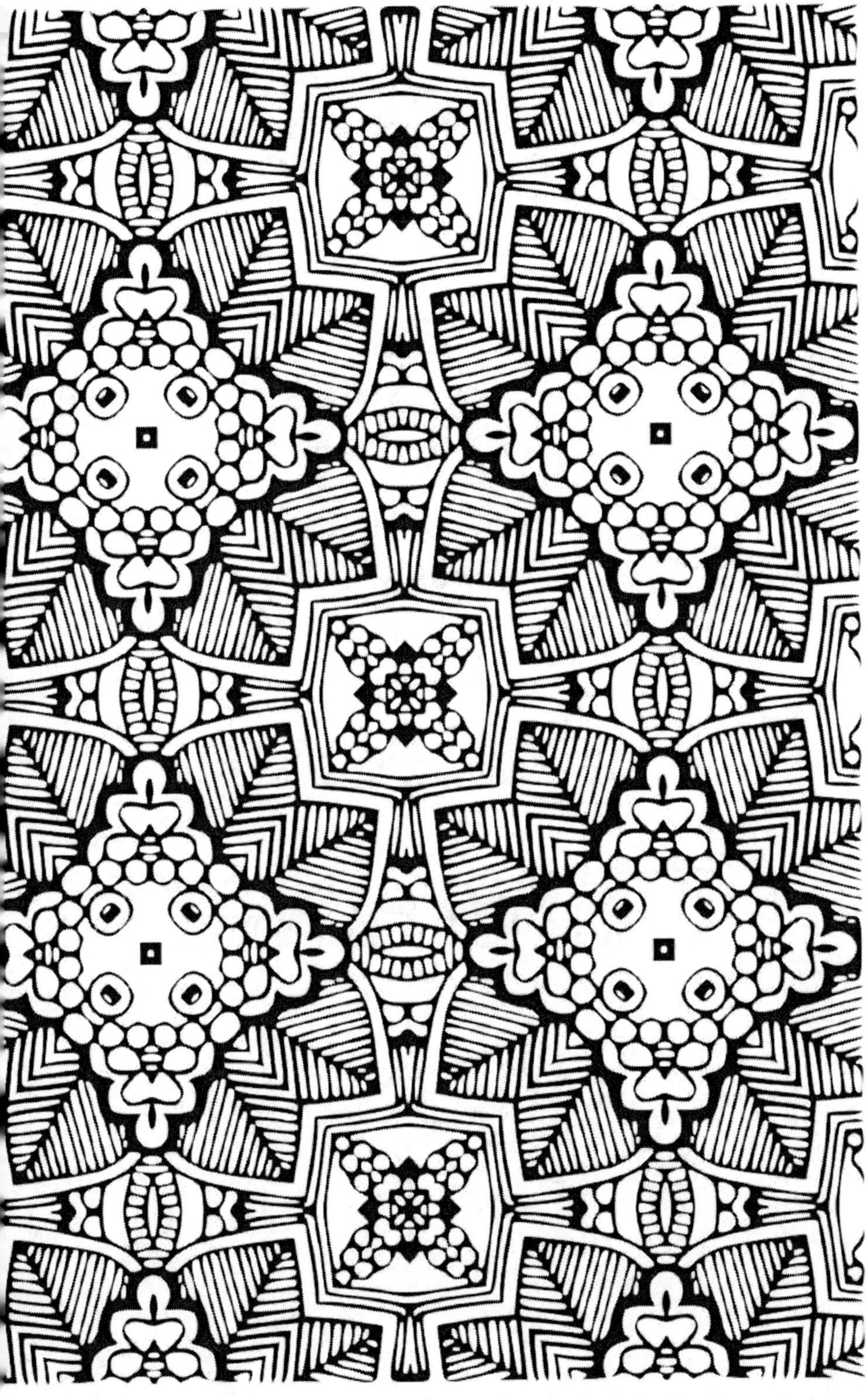

Think Positive

Positive Things will happen.

# write it down

What are you holding on to that you need to let go of?

If "Plan A" didn't work. The alphabet has 25 more letters.

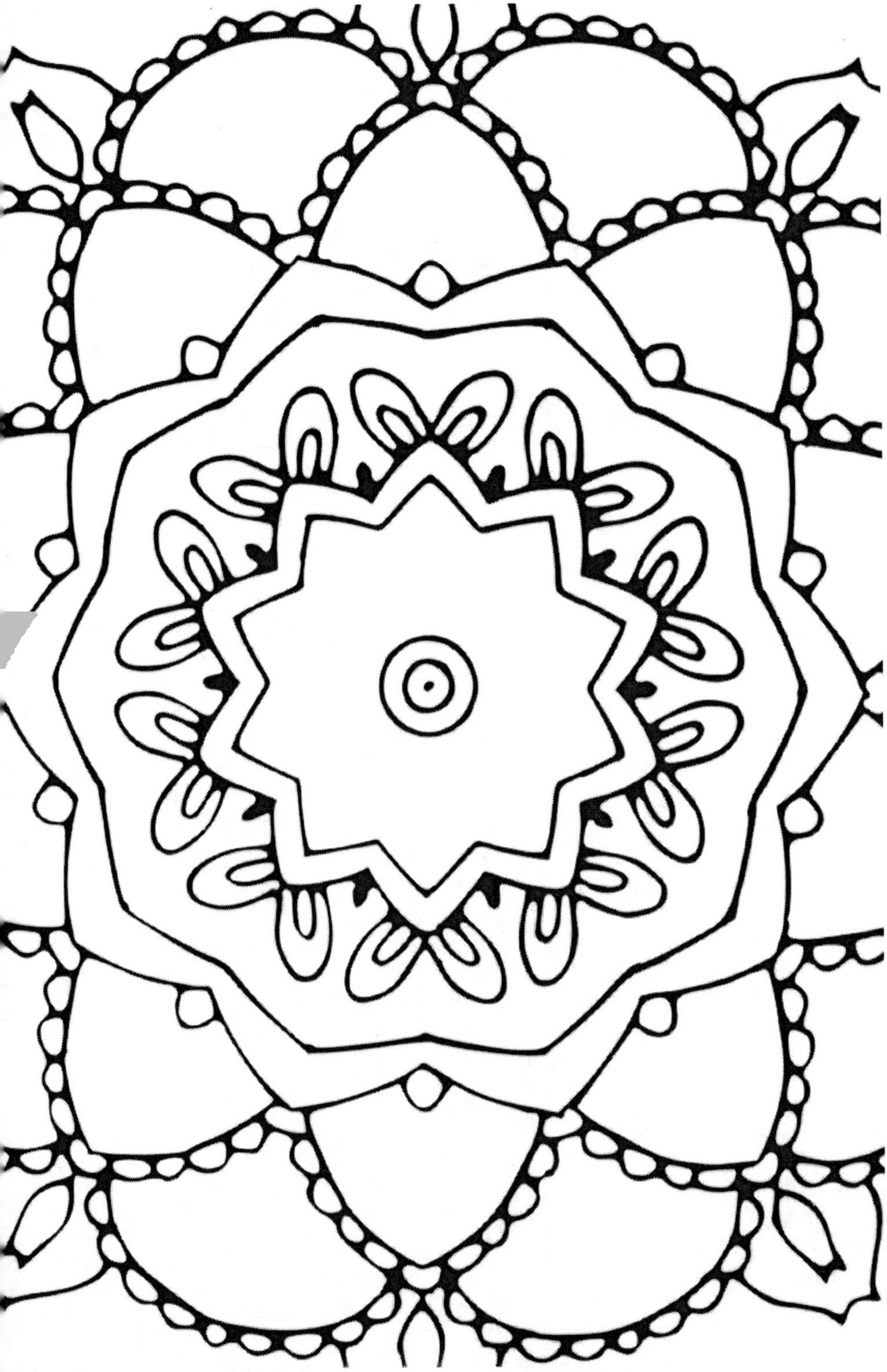

# BELIEVE YOU CAN AND YOU WILL.

# write it down

List the first 6 things you do when you wake up in the morning. Do these activities pave the way for success in your life? If no, what do you need to change about your morning routine?

# Woman

# I

# AM

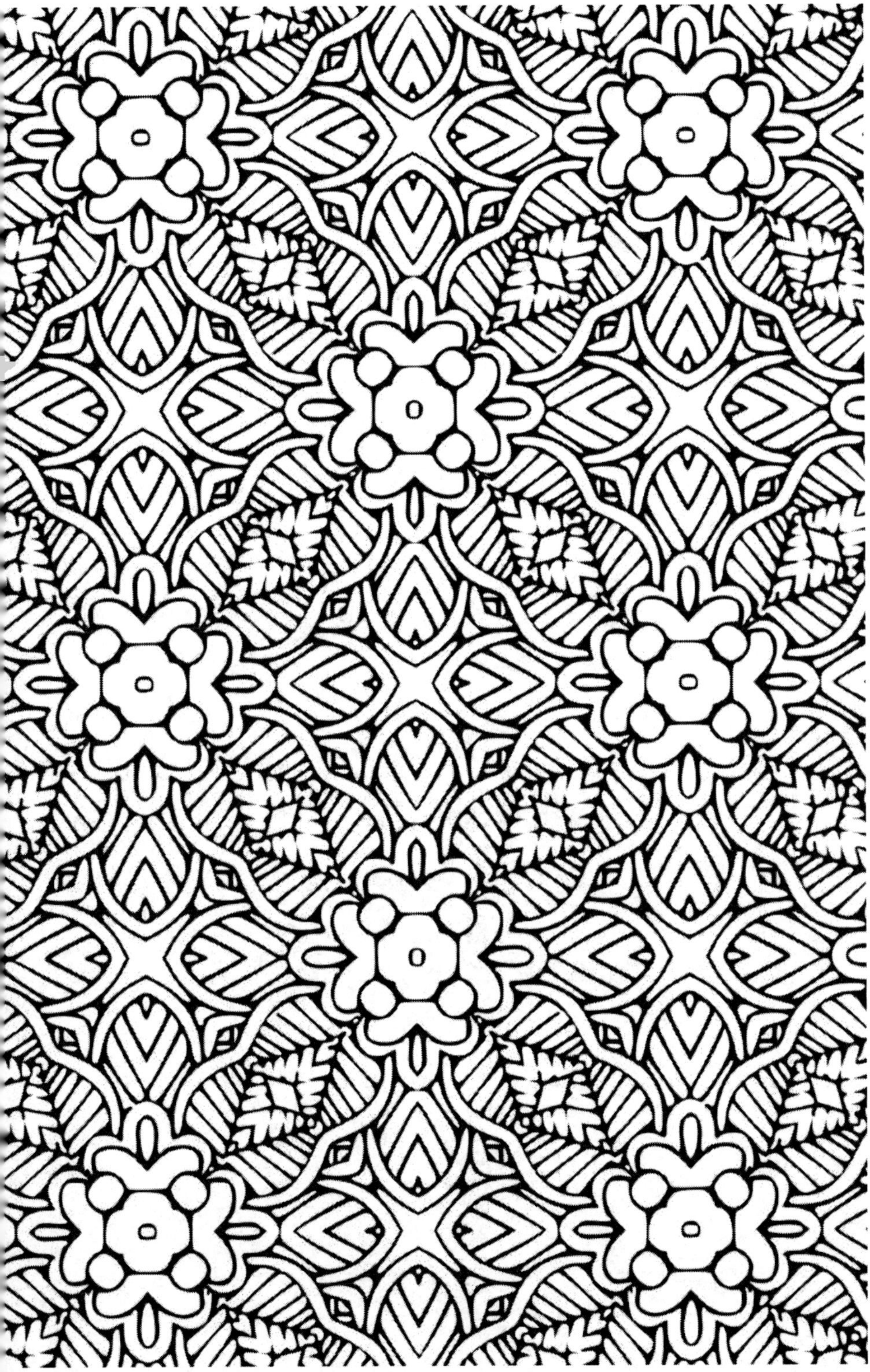

BE SCARED

AND

DO THE

DAMN THING

ANYWAY.

# write it down

## Who am I?

*be you.*
*do you.*
*for you.*

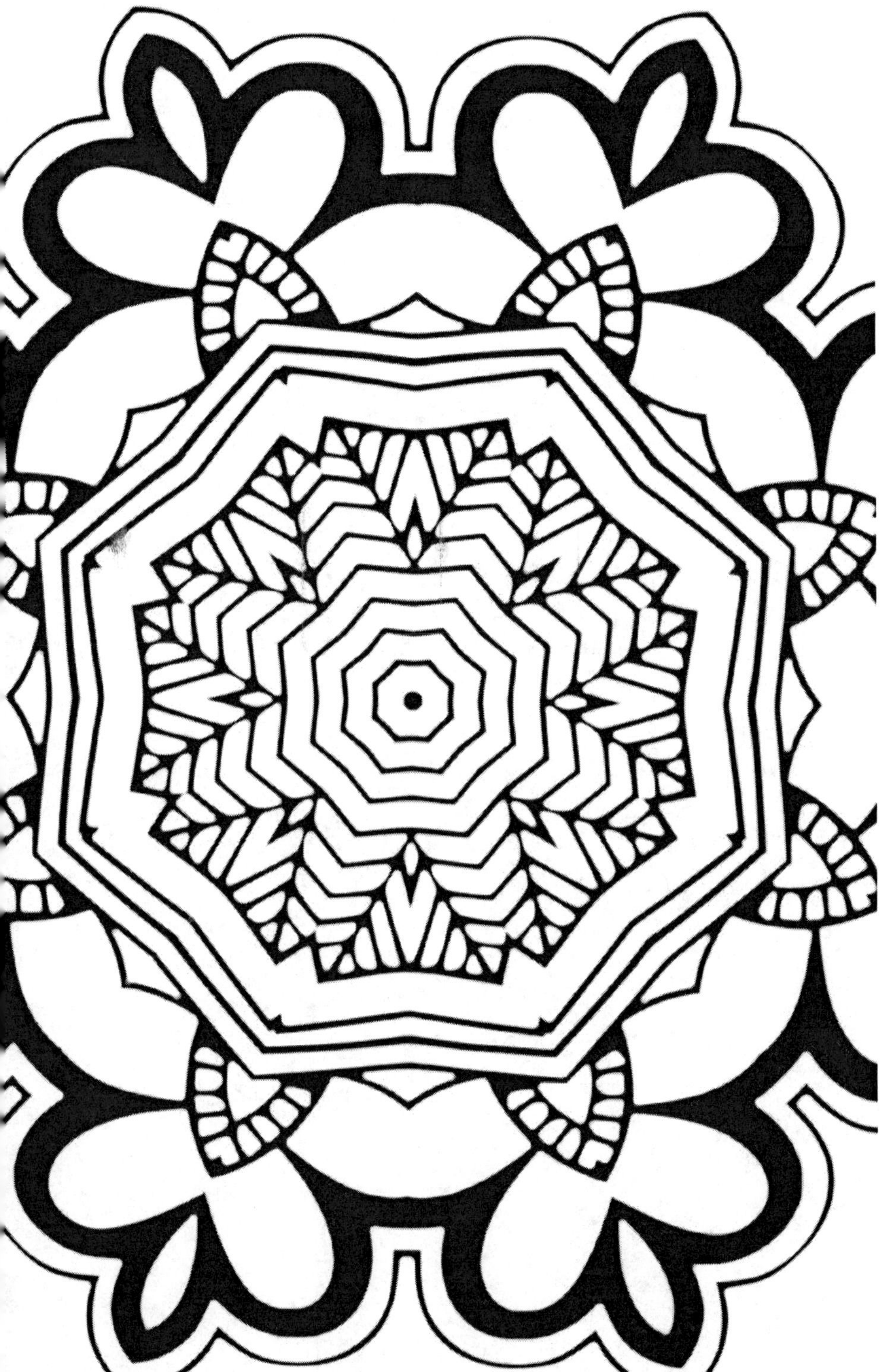

COLORS

speak

LOUDER

than

WORDS

# write it down

List the ways you love to have fun.

# BE

# KINDNESS is free. SPRINKLE THAT SHIT EVERYWHERE!

# write it down

Am I doing what I love? If yes, what does that look like? If no, why not?

:(:

you decide.

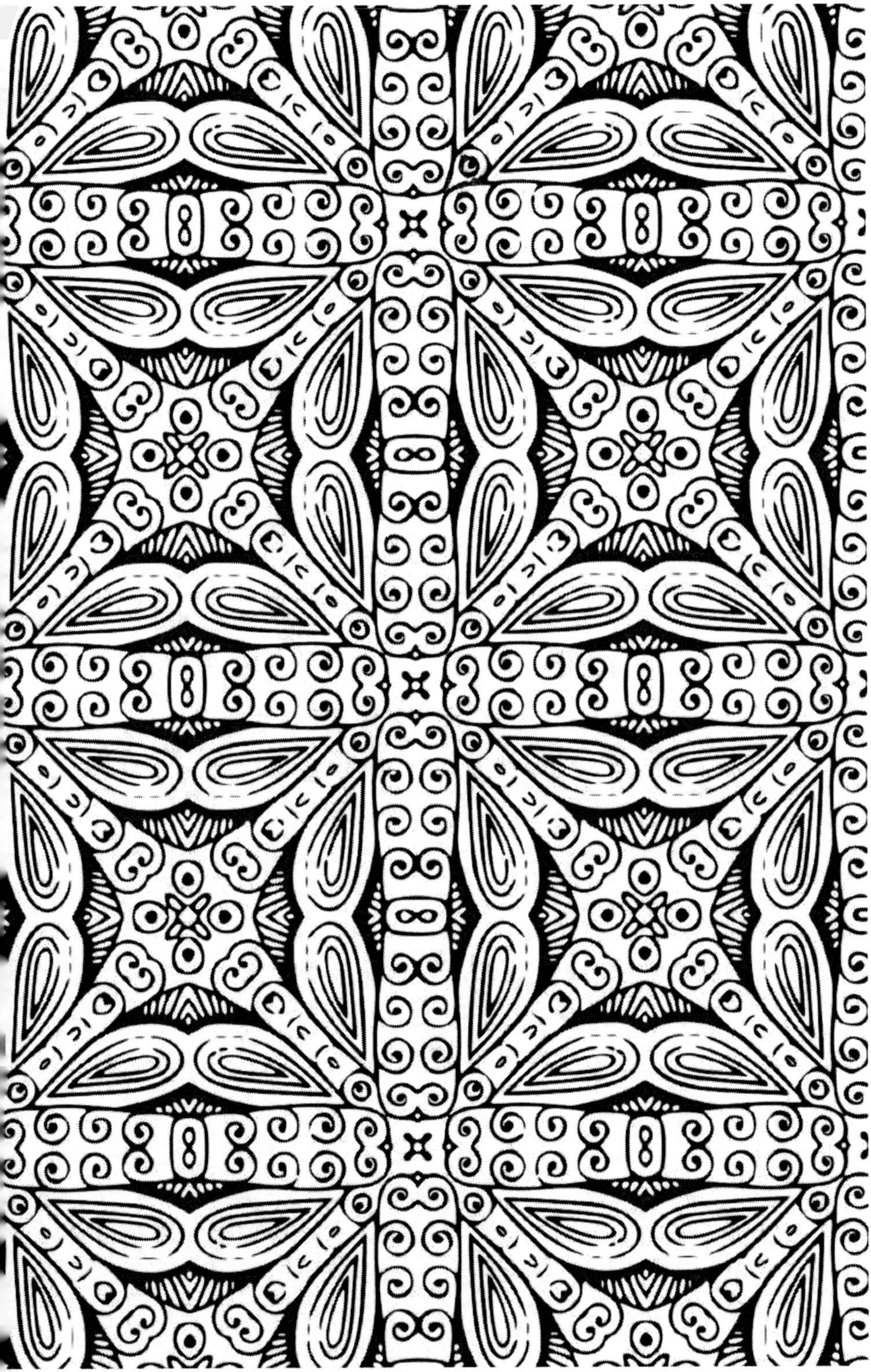

*and so the adventure begins*

# write it down

What is your most favorite place on earth? Why?

# NEVER REGRET ANYTHING

# BREAK OUT OF YOUR COMFORT ZONE AND SHINE BRIGHTER!

# write it down

How do you live your life out loud?

# LISA RENEE JOHNSON

Lisa Renee is a bestselling fiction author, sought-after speaker, and certified professional coach. Her mission is to help others create an amazing life and shine from the inside out. Through workshops and training programs, she teaches individuals to get unstuck in life and their book business. She is the founder and Chief Sunshineologist of I Got Sunshine and the Sunshine Success Circle, both communities for women to thrive and unleash the shine within and The Bestseller Game Plan, a workshop intensive for authors to create a marketing strategy to fuel higher profits in their book business.

Lisa Renee also captured the country's attention with the hashtag #laughingwhileblack that ignited a media firestorm and prompted global conversations about power, privilege and racial bias. Lisa Renee inspires individuals to shed their excuses, live life out loud, and to define success and happiness on their own terms.

information can be obtained
w.ICGtesting.com
l in the USA
01n0103060218
S

CPS
at w
Prin
FSO
4419